Search for Significance

Herbert M Barber, Jr, PhD, PhD

Herbert M Barber, Jr, PhD, PhD

September 2017, revision 1
February 2016, original publication

To Daddy

Herbert M. Barber, Sr.

A man of significance.

Herbert M Barber, Jr, PhD, PhD

This is God's universe, and he does things his way.
You may have a better way, but you don't have a universe.

J. Vernon McGee, Th.D.

Herbert M Barber, Jr, PhD, PhD

Foreword

My spiritual role model is my Granddaddy. In my opinion, he is the definition of a Godly man. Whether serving as a deacon in his church, serving my Grandmamma every day, or just greeting everyone with sincere kindness, he is selfless. Growing up watching and learning from him has given me the moral compass that I strive to live by today. Even with all the wisdom he has, he still remains a humble man. He stays in the background, never drawing attention to himself, but always serving. The funny thing is, I guess, my dad says I am growing up to be just like Granddaddy. How could I ask for a greater compliment?

Brandon H Barber, 20
February 13, 2016

It seems that so many people want to be praised today for their accomplishments, but as for Granddaddy, he never seeks praise from anyone. I guess that's because, to him, he has never worked a day in his life, especially since retiring. He just "piddles," whether helping Grandmama, we grandchildren, or anyone else. Everything he does seems to be an attempt to make the lives of everyone else better, even if at his expense.

He has taught me many things over the years: courage, honesty, integrity, humility, kindness, and of course, hard work. And it seems so rare today to find someone as dedicated to their spouse as Granddaddy is to Grandmama. He has such a giving heart, especially to her. He not only treats her with love and respect, he also treats his family and others with love and respect, so much so that over the years I have grown so fond of the way he treats Grandmama that I hope to marry a young man just like him some day.

Natalie M Barber, 17
February 13, 2016

Herbert M Barber, Jr, PhD, PhD

Search for Significance

Herbert M Barber, Jr, PhD, PhD

Preface

As these words are penned, my children are 20 and 17; one is a United States Marine, and one is a junior in high school. From an eternal perspective, I am only a few years older than them, yet the world I have known, they will never know. They will never know the feel of wet tobacco leaves slapping them in the face in the early morning, the sweltering heat of a tobacco field at midday, nor the joy of racking the last rack of tobacco for the day. They will never know the freedom of riding your bicycle across town to attend what we now call middle school, or the relief associated with dodging big dogs along the way. They will never know the voice of their mother calling them home from three blocks away for dinner, nor what it is like to stomp through the snake-infested branch that leads home. Neither will they understand how we functioned in a day with no air conditioner, cell phone, or computer.

Then again, I will never know many things my father knows, like delivering newspapers on your bike in the dark hours before school, or taking a biscuit to school for lunch. I will never know what it is like to help your mother wash laundry by hand for a family of ten, and I will never know what it is like to pick cotton by hand, wear hand-me-down clothes that were threadbare two kids back, or hope to receive an orange or apple for Christmas. Nor will I ever know the freedom that comes with hitchhiking home from New York to South Georgia after serving in the US Army in Germany, nor what it is like to house, feed, and clothe a young family of five on less than realistic rations.

I guess the times as they say, well, they are a changin'. No longer is catching crawfish in the branch down the road enough to maintain a child's attention all day. No longer is the football game Friday night the community event we plan for all week, and no longer is the children's Christmas musical at church the big event of the year. Yes, indeed, times have changed, and America has changed along with it.

I suppose change is inevitable. For persons over 40, 50, or so, we have witnessed an explosion of intellectual, technological, political, social, and economic change as never before in America or elsewhere. Along with those changes, we have experienced many, many successes as a nation. Today, we are a very sophisticated society, and I might add, a very savvy society. By every measure, we are the greatest nation in the history of humankind. There is nothing we do not have, yet young entrepreneurs regularly develop things we never knew we needed. Then we cannot function without them.

However, material success often runs counter to spiritual success; in fact, the relationship is usually inverse. As our material success increases, our spiritual success decreases; and conversely, as our material success decreases, our spiritual success increases. No matter, the polarity between these two variables keeps us off balance individually and collectively as we strive to serve two masters. Inevitably we find ourselves caught in a vicious cycle between mandates dictated by the two masters, and in the confusion we lose sight of who we are as individuals, and moreover, whose we are. Yet we plug along trying to be all we can be so we too can be seen as significant.

Unfortunately, in our attempt to serve two masters, our search to accomplish something of importance, to be somebody more, to be significant, is challenged, right up until it no longer seems enough to be one after God's own heart, to be one of his chosen.

Using primarily Moses, Job, and Joseph as instruments in our discussion regarding significance, multiple issues are addressed herein, most of which is for seasoned Christians who God has called to deeper relationships with him. In so doing, a few central themes run throughout this discussion, with these themes addressed over and over as they occur in the lives of these men. But while these themes may be only somewhat implicit, they are obvious to the discerning Christian. Of course, the struggles these men faced in their oscillating strides for some resemblance of significance is then paralleled with struggles deeply committed Christians face as God shapes them for deeper relationships with him. Through it all, this examination is not for the weak in spirit, but for the weathered Christian who has somehow managed to remain faithful to God despite struggles to the contrary.

To this end, I have taken every effort to make the content easy to follow and worth following, simultaneously. For me, writings such as these are awkward undertakings, as in these type writings the message is better conveyed in conversational tone, where strong sentence structure and grammar is thrown by the wayside to convey one's central thesis. Such simply runs counter to thirty-three years of formal education. Nonetheless, it is my sincere desire that you prayerfully consider the words written as you ponder your own search for significance.

When God Calls

Outside of grace, arguably, nothing life offers supersedes God's call. Not fortune, not fame, nor what they bring. In most cases, fortune and fame prove juxtaposed to the daily grind of his call.

A s a child, my sisters and I often stayed with a deeply committed Christian while our parents worked. She and her husband scraped by on the meager rations they earned logging, babysitting, and ironing. Neither could read nor write, and neither could drive. Of course, driving would have been of limited value as they certainly never had the financial means to purchase a vehicle.

They lived in an old house supported on loosely placed brick piers that made for uneven floors. Located on the edge of the woods on a dirt road, just off the paved road, their house had a tin roof, no air conditioning, and no central heat. But many great days were spent swinging on Mrs. Murphy's front porch as we listened to her hum old hymns. Even now, I can feel the breeze across my damp face as I listen to her hum *Amazing Grace* while waiting on Mr. Murphy, or Papa as we called him, to return from his walk to Alfred's or Red & White Supermarket with a single paper bag of groceries filled with a few sausage links, lima beans, rice, and most importantly, cracklin' for homemade cornbread. Even the smallest portion of this meal was certain to send your heart into overdrive.

Certainly, we will never forget those days, her, nor the lessons learned. Mrs. Murphy influenced our lives in ways only God himself could have orchestrated. To this day, I will never forget how to collect eggs—or catch a chicken for lunch—nor the deeper lessons associated with Godly living.

Her neighbor, also an older woman and committed Christian, walked down the little dirt road to Mrs. Murphy's house on a regular basis to read the Bible and Sunday school lesson aloud to her. Week in and week out, rain or shine, Mrs. Gertie was there to read God's word to one who could not.

Saints such as these will be far ahead of most of us in Heaven, and their crowns will be many. For some, like Mrs. Murphy and Mrs. Gertie, serving God comes through simple acts of obedience. Reading to someone who cannot, caring for an elderly friend, or comforting a wayward child. For others, heeding God's call proves to be an arduous undertaking, one that requires perseverance found only through his grace.

For example, many pastors needlessly suffer at the hands of other Christians, and conversely, many Christians needlessly suffer at the hands of pastors. Some Christians suffer at the hands of non-Christians, and additionally, some non-Christians suffer at the hands of Christians. This is life in "Christian" America today. Sadly, "Out of one hundred men, one will read the Bible, the other ninety-nine will read the Christian."[1]

Earlier in my career, God led me to leave my career doing engineering and economic analysis on complex mega-projects with the largest engineering firm in the world to design and build churches. A noble feat, one might say, but to me professionally, it would serve as a small smudge on my career. The work itself was

---

[1] D.L. Moody

easy. The people were not. The planning was easy. The financial analysis was easy. Any type of rudimentary decision modeling was easy. The architecture and engineering was easy, and the construction was easy. More often than not, however, the people with whom we worked, including pastors, bishops, staff, deacons, and members, were backstabbing, manipulative, ungrateful, self-centered, untruthful, and unethical. They cheated us at every available opportunity, and then some. They created opportunities to cheat us. More often than not, they made what should have been wonderful experiences almost dreadful.

They schemed. They stole money from us, literally. They withheld money though they knew it was due. They knowingly lied—again. They were corrupt. They were malicious. They expected everything for free, despite us already having given them tens and even hundreds of thousands of dollars of work and cash at no charge to them. Deacons worked behind the scenes to successfully thwart building programs. Even building committee chairs led efforts to halt building programs from moving forward, as did many pastors. Pastors lied to their congregations, they lied to their bankers, and they lied to us. Churches blamed everyone but themselves for being over budget despite the obvious. They left my firm hanging on millions of dollars, never paying what they were contractually bound to pay. During my brief tenure on this noble cause, we were forced to file lawsuits on several occasions, many of which were in small towns with judges who were completely lost in terms of simple cost accounting, and even basic contractual law. Just lost. Yes, seriously. Frankly, dealing with such gross incompetence and ignorance was intellectually, emotionally, and spiritually draining. They sucked the life from me and everyone who worked with these churches. But make no mistake about it; we were a Godsend to these people. Just ask them. Right up until they had to pay our first invoice.

I had a successful career in the making; why would God call now? Committees regularly bore false witness against us, despite knowing the truth. Oh, they never complained regarding the quality of our work, nor the performance thereof, but they complained about everything else. They fussed to everyone who would listen. Their friends, congregations, committee members, pastors, and denominational leaders. The building committees fought with the finance committee, the finance committee fought with the deacons and board, the deacons and board fought with the pastor, and the pastor completed the circle by fighting with the building committee. And guess who was caught in the middle of their vicious cycle. We took the blame for every evil act, despite signed documentation to the contrary. Perhaps worse than anything, the churches we served were simply a very ungrateful people. Not every person, and not every church certainly, but overall, they were ungrateful. And in the middle of a perfectly good career, God thought it would be a good idea for me to work with these people.

Honestly, I think Satan was happiest when we were helping churches. Oh, not because he greedily rubbed his hands together in wait to ambush us with the evils associated with each church. No, churches were masters at rendering greed, ungratefulness, and ill-will against us. Satan was happiest during these projects because he could relax a minute, maybe take a vacation. God's people were doing his work.

Perhaps a little color commentary will add clarity to how ridiculous it was trying to help churches; and recall, I had given up a real career with smart people to help "these people."[2] And while a couple of these examples are humorous, they all sum up the incompetence, ignorance, and ungratefulness of it all.

---

[2] Yes; after all these years, my emotions regarding this topic are alive and well.

1. I struggled that day to juggle my travel schedule to make a 6:00pm meeting with a church in Tupelo, Mississippi, but after stumbling from bed at 4:00am that morning from a hotel in some state I do not recall, where I had returned around midnight following last night's meeting, I managed to make it through my typical day of dealing with delayed flights, sold-out car rental agencies, no-vacancy hotels, and the other normalcies that had long been my life. I had made it. Six sharp; close, but just in time for yet another presentation. But twenty minutes into what should be a three-hour meeting, a lady rushed into the meeting exclaiming, "This meeting has to be quick. I have hand bells at 6:30, and I have to eat dinner before that, too." And she did exactly as she suggested. The new facilities were never constructed.

2. After holding several meetings and developing numerous conceptual designs and cost estimates with a church in Tuscaloosa, Alabama, the long-awaited vote to proceed with their building program had arrived. Their new facilities would be beautiful,

and better, the church fully supported the building program. Today was merely for the record. Immediately prior to a vote that day, a former deacon of the church who had not attended church in years, mandated to be heard. And as he rambled, the pastor began to chime in his two cents, the same pastor who, 10 minutes before was a huge proponent of the building program. Then a current deacon, followed by a couple in the congregation offered their wisdom. Within 20 minutes, a man who had not attended church in years talked a congregation of 700 into not building the new facilities they so badly needed. The church never built.

3. During what was a pleasant meeting with a church in Metter, Georgia, where "everything is better in Metter," a committee member interrupted us in the middle of our presentation, and in a loud, authoritative voice, told us we were "idiots" who just wanted to "rip them off." Even after his sincere apology the following day, we chose to never return.

Of course, all these years later they have never built the new facilities they needed.

4. The executive vice president of the local bank in small Manchester, Georgia served as the chair of the building program at the church we were building. In her words, she told me she was "a numbers person," and as long as it dealt with numbers, especially finance, she could help the building committee and congregation understand it. So, as with likely every contract I have signed over the course of 30 years, their contract had a clause stating that we would charge 18 percent per annum for monies past due on a pro-rated basis. Of course, when we charged her church that same 1.5 percent for paying late that month, she made a fool of herself as she authoritatively exclaimed that she had *never* heard of a company charging interest for late payment. Well, apparently she wasn't the sharpest tool in the shed when it came to "numbers," after all. Perhaps she should ask her boss how she gets paid.

5. A building committee member on this same small church project in Manchester, Georgia demonstrated his deep knowledge of engineering as he literally yelled at us during a monthly meeting, stating that the concrete in the floor slab had cracks "all over the place." Among other things, he excitedly informed us as only his 21 years of infinite wisdom could, that he was a "certified utility worker," whatever that is, and that, "when 'done right,' concrete 'don't' crack." After being able to take his rant no further, I let the drag off my line and let him run like a fish stealing my bait, and the more he mouthed off, the farther I let him run, right up until I reared back and set the hook. "Well, now, how bad were these cracks, Robert; I mean, did they run all the way across that section of the building?" "Oh, yea!" he proudly stated. "Yes, they did! Alllll... the way across. Cracks are everywhere!" "And, did they not only run all the way across the building, but did they occur, at like 20 feet on center, like at every column line?" I asked. And as he exclaimed, "Yes, yes! Yes, they did! And when done right, concrete don't crack," another member on their building

committee stopped him cold. "Shut up, Robert. You sound like an idiot. After 40 years in the construction industry, I have never seen a concrete slab that did *not* crack. These cracks are from them forcing the expansion and contraction in the concrete to occur on 20-foot centers with expansion joints. Just sit there and be quiet." Oh, and yes; this kid's mother was the "numbers person" noted above. Apparently, genius ran in the family.

6. Toward the end of a building program for a new educational building in St. Marys, Georgia, I privately handed the pastor a personal check for $50,000, asking him to put this money toward reaching others for Christ. His very sincere comment said it all. "Well, I appreciate it and all, but you just overcharged us in the first place; then wrote us a check for $50,000." I wish I had that money today; I would blow it on wasteful things in his name.

7. A pastor and his church in Madray Springs, just outside of Jesup, Georgia, refused to pay us on a cost-plus contract because their wants began to

exceed their ability to pay. As Daddy used to say growing up, "They got a little too big for their britches." Despite their attorneys advising them to the contrary, that they owned the money, and us forking out over $150,000 in legal fees for our attorney to tell them the same, they still refused to pay us. "Just because." After all, as I have learned over the years, "just because" always serves the ignorant and ill-intended well. And after the small-town judge in a preliminary hearing stated in open court that our firm was "not entitled to collect overhead" on any costs associated with the project, we made the decision to drop the suit, altogether. Besides, if the presiding judge was this incompetent, imagine what a jury of our "peers" would have looked like. And moreover, in the unlikely event that we would have convinced a judge and jury through the very basics of business, cost accounting, and contract law, how would we actually collect? Today this church owes me $1.2 million, and until they pay it, I still own a portion of their worship center. The pastor, committee chair, and building committee know they owe it, but no worries for stealing these monies from me; they are covered by the blood. That's okay. However, one of these days I am going to go off the deep end and buy up all the property adjacent to their country church, move in a bunch of half-vacant 1970s vintage single-wide mobile homes, and put in a small hog farm just upwind from their (my) worship center. "Just because."

8. The pastor of a church we were building in Milledgeville, Georgia, the former capital of Georgia, lied to his 700-member congregation, telling them their banker refused to loan them additional monies to pay for their cost overruns because we were over-charging them. After we produced signed documentation by their pastor to the congregation and banker the following week, the pastor crawled back to me in a Crackle Barrel, not to apologize, but to ask me to finance the $510,000 in change orders they owed us. Oh yea; I jumped right on that one.

9. A pastor and committee member in a church in the one-horse town of Bronwood, Georgia claimed we overcharged them a whopping $7,000 on their

project, and filed a complaint not through the civil court system but as a *criminal* case brought through a district attorney so the church could receive free legal counseling. Finally, after spending over $90,000 in legal and accounting fees, my firm was completely exonerated from such stupidity. Yep, you can bet these people are on my annual Christmas card list.

Thank God; my stint trying to serve God's churches was brief. The ungratefulness was overwhelming. And worse, these few examples represent merely of a handful of churches who, to this day, still owe me money, personally. And be reminded, there is no difference between what these churches did and *stealing*. So, what happened to the corrupt pastors, deacons, and members? Nothing; not a single repercussion, but apparently God felt it was a good idea for me to experience such, right in the middle of a perfectly good career. Eventually I gave up altogether on the idea of helping churches.

In fact, over the course of 30 years of experience as an expert in engineering economic systems on often very complex and contentious projects with billions of dollars at stake, the lying, stealing, and corruption associated with my stint with pastors, staff members, deacons, boards, committees, and church members far surpassed even the worst person with whom I have dealt on large projects in industry and infrastructure—projects, mind you, that are some 1,000, 2,000, 3,000, even 10,000 or 20,000 times more expensive than the average church project; projects that not only affect a few hundred people at a time, or even a few generations thereafter; but projects that affect entire countries, and even entire world markets—for generations, where erroneous or weak calculations, poor decisions, and recommendations on my part may completely wipe out regions of the economy in the US, and simultaneously the economies of entire countries.

It is sad, however. It is very sad; for contrary to what you think, behind the scenes in churches, it can be unnecessarily ugly. The ignorance coupled with greed, selfishness, and pride is damning. I guess A. W. Tozer was right. "One hundred religious persons knit into a unity by careful organization do not constitute a church any more than eleven dead men make a football team," at least not as God intended.

Of course, the irony we realize after following God's will in what we envision as ill-advised endeavors is that his will is most often different than what we initially envision, far different. We are always building up, and God is always tearing down. Think about it. How many pastors feel called to a smaller church with a smaller salary and less recognition; I can't name one. The higher the income and the more the notoriety, the stronger "the call." However, you can believe that God holistically calls people to serve him without regard to what it does to their financial livelihood, recognition, and notoriety. But like pastors, we all remain vigilant in our attempts to increase while God is busy decreasing. In the end, God's will is more about yielding, and less about *doing*.

I learned this lesson very early in my career, albeit in a different setting with a different outcome. I had just graduated from college with my undergraduate degree in engineering and had several offers on the table, none which were in my preferred location of Atlanta. One of the last offers I received was to work as a cost engineer for a large company in Greenville, South Carolina, a small southern city housing several very large engineering firms.

The starting salary for young engineers in the mid-1980's averaged $22,000-24,000 a year on a good day, and of the four or five offers under consideration, they ranged from $20,000 a year to $25,000 a year. So, you can imagine my surprise when this company in Greenville offered me $32,000 a year, plus benefits and all the other trimmings a 22-year-old could never appreciate. But $32,000 a year! That was something to consider. It was some $10,000 more than my friends were being offered.

But wait a minute; I was well established in my walk with Christ, I thought. I better pray about this thing. So, I prayed earnestly regarding this offer. But after all, it was so much money; it had to be God's will. What a huge blessing! I could see it now. Never again would I have to live in a dumpy apartment with a wrecked car that set more than it ran. Never again would I have to ride my bicycle an hour across town to go to the grocery store or class just because my transportation refused to transport.

But after anxiously praying the decision over a couple of days and talking it over with my parents, I knew this position was not for me. A great opportunity, a solid job, and a huge company. Nonetheless, I felt no peace in accepting. Oh, God was in it, alright; he just had no interest in my accepting.

So, I hesitantly made the phone call to respectfully decline their offer. Before I finished declining their offer, however, they said they had been thinking about it and felt I was worth more than they offered given that I had acquired a few years of experience while in college working on a large stay-cabled suspension bridge project. After all, I was a mere 19-22 years old at the time, and my responsibilities were to conduct the trigonometry calculations necessary to ensure that horizontal and vertical control were maintained during construction. In so doing, I was responsible for ensuring that the towers on each side of the river, along with the main span and all approach bents and associated ramps, aligned to the nth degree in terms of angle and distance, whether 50 feet underground or dangling over 500 feet above the water surface under conditions that OSHA, or any sane person, would not describe as *safe* then, let alone today. In lay terms, my responsibility was to ensure that the bridge people drive over today actually met in the middle of the river. So, I suppose given that I had managed to acquire a little solid experience and responsibility already, they reconsidered their offer.

Who knows what caused them to reconsider, but they did. I still recall that conversation as if it were yesterday. "So, we want to up our offer from $32,000 a year to $34,000 a year." What?! What was I to do now? The original offer was much higher than anyone with whom I graduated, and now they wanted to "up their offer?" Wow! God must really be in this thing! After all; I mean, I called to decline their offer and they raised the stakes associated with my declining. Who does that to a kid? Indeed, this must be a God-thing. "And if $34,000 a year is not enough to entice you, I can probably get you a little more, maybe $37,000." Wow! This *was* a God-thing!

I had my eye on a new car, a Nissan Maxima, or actually, anything that ran. I could hear the purr of the engine now. Ahhh, the sweet sound of an engine that actually ran. One hundred and fifty-two horsepower of pure pleasure. A fraction of the horsepower I would one-day wheel, but today? Priceless.

But I turned down their offer. Flatly. Right then and there, I turned it down. No second guessing. I had prayed about it, and God had answered. God had directed, and I had followed. The decision was made. God had no interest in me accepting this offer in Greenville, even if it was with one of the largest engineering firms in the world, and even if it came with the answer to my transportation dreams. He only wanted me to obey.

Suffice it to say, how I felt would not exactly qualify as happy, but I obeyed nonetheless. I guess he never said I had to actually like his will. As A.W. Tozer surmised, "The true Christian ideal is not to be happy, but to be holy." Well, I must have thought, I will just settle for being holy.

After making that dreadful decision that Friday morning, I sat dejected in my apartment all weekend. Half mad, half pouting, and half sad; but fully faithful. My dreams of starting my life as a young adult and having that nice car were snatched from me. I struggled, but I rested knowing my decision was his decision.

That Sunday afternoon I prayed, "God, I know this was your will, and I want to follow you, but I have struggled financially so long to get through college. It has taken five and a half years to make it through the last four. I was just hoping life would get a little easier one day..." Then the deafening ring from the telephone startled me. Remember when a phone was a phone? When we had real rings, not the sissy rings of today?

"Mr. Barber, I am with a small engineering consulting firm in Greenville, South Carolina, and I would like to discuss the possibility of your coming to work with our firm, not in Greenville, but in Atlanta."

Atlanta! Wow! I was surprised, but remember, I was still in mourning recovering from my let-down on Friday. Like all overcomers of misfortune, however, I said, "Sure. I would love to meet with you."

So, following our initial meeting in the parking lot of a closed restaurant in Augusta, Georgia, I was invited to interview in Atlanta with senior engineers from Atlanta and Chicago. It was then that I really began to feel God leading toward this company. From the first phone call and meeting in Augusta, we all seemed to have a kindred spirit, if you will. We just fit. Following that interview, I then went to Greenville to interview. It was there that we would begin salary discussions, if there were to be any. And mind you; I was 22 years old at the time. What did I know about negotiations? I knew everything of nothing, so when asked what I wanted I confidently threw out a ridiculous number. "$40,000 a year!" So what if it was nearly twice the average starting salary for a young engineer, or more than twice as much as all other college majors. What were they going to say; no? So, what? It was not my first-time hearing "no" in life. I had heard it many times in my young life.

But after hearing my number, they did not budge. Not a "no;" not even a chuckle. Heck, not even an "Ohhh-kay..." But while leaving their office that afternoon, my soon-to-be boss told me he thought he could get me not my ridiculous salary requirement of $40,000 a year but the outlandish number of $54,000 a year! I just stood there, stunned, as a hush fell about the place. What was I to say? I was speechless. I was just there, suspended between reality and a dream. And as I stood in my shocked state of lifeless ambiguity with my eyes glossing over with tears, my soon-to-be boss told me he would call me Sunday night with their final offer, slapped me on the back, and said, "Have a safe trip home."

Overcome with God's goodness, I prayed all the way home. I could talk with no one. No such thing then as cell phones, thank God. Just the hum of the road, me... and God. So, I rambled on and on thanking him immensely for the lessons he had taught me regarding obedience. As I was soon to learn however, this little lesson on obedience wasn't over; far from it.

So, I anxiously waited for my phone to ring Sunday night, and I prayed. I remember it as if it were yesterday. "God, I am so blown away; I don't know what to say. I just want to follow you, God. I no longer care. Your will, God; not mine." Then the phone rang. "Herb, this is Tony." And after about 15 minutes of chitchat, Tony laid their final offer on the table. "Our people in Atlanta and Chicago loved you; so did our people in Greenville. You bring a lot to the table as a young man, and this is a great opportunity for you. Pray over it; we need your decision tomorrow. Our offer is $72,000 a year. Call me tomorrow, buddy. Good night."

And as then, I don't know what to say today, either; their offer is equivalent to offering a young college kid with minimal experience $164,000 today.[3] Ironically, some thirty years have passed since that day, and my reflections regarding these events are as vivid now as they were that day. Yes, indeed, it was a God-thing. And the truth be told, perhaps the real blessing only came today as I revisited the story with you of God teaching a kid one of his first lessons regarding spiritual obedience.

---

[3] 2016 USD

Not all stories have happy endings, of course. Not yours; not mine. But God calls, nonetheless. For some, accepting God's call requires them to embrace life under circumstances that mandate extreme sacrifices. For some forty years, Lottie Moon sacrificed a relatively comfortable life as a teacher in America to meet the physical and spiritual needs of the people of Communist China, only to eventually die of starvation. More recently, Kim Dong-shik, a Christian minister who established underground shelters in China for fleeing North Korean refugees, was tortured and starved after being captured by the North Korean government. [4, 5] And of course, more recently more and more Christians are being beheaded in the Middle East because they refuse to deny Christ.

Moses too would learn the challenges associated with accepting God's call on his life, and the immense struggles found in doing so. Before his life was over, Moses would fully comprehend the wisdom found only through a lifetime of self-denial. Perhaps such would never be so driven home as when

---

[4] In 2015, Rev. Lee was awarded $330 million by the North Korean government for their government's role in his kidnapping, imprisonment, and torture. *Reverend Kim Dong Shik's family awarded $330 million in case against North Korean government*. Christianity Today, 2015).

[5] International Christian Concern, Persecution, 2013.

after leading God's people out of bondage, after following God's call, he was denied entrance into the Promised Land.

Then again, many will never appreciate God's call, for most will never accept it. Even fewer will appreciate blessing as God intended, blessing that can only be found through complete denial of self. "That which you sow does not come to life unless it dies..." (1 Corinthians 1:33) Not my will but *his* will. Perhaps Henry Blackaby is right. "The problem with Christian leaders is not that they don't know what God wants them to do. They problem is... they are unwilling to do it."

Consider the challenges associated with Moses merely accepting God's call. First, it came from nowhere. As the flames engulfed the bush, God confirms who he is to Moses, "I am the God of your father, the God of Abraham, the God of Isaac, and the God of Jacob." (Exodus 3:6) After telling Moses who he was and why he was there, God charged him. "Therefore, come now, and I will send you to Pharaoh, so that you may bring my people, the sons of Israel, out of Egypt." (Exodus 3:9) There was no small talk. There was no initial discussion; there was no, "There is something I have been meaning to talk with you about, Moses. Come sit beside the fire." Nothing.

No doubt for years Moses' relationship with God had been rocky; up and down, as he relived his past of doing what he thought was right. After all, killing an evil man intent on destroying one of God's own perhaps has merit. And for this, for doing what many Christians would consider right, his blessing became forty years of essentially nothingness. Absolutely nothing; he lost everything. Perhaps even his relationship with God, at least to what it may have been in years' past.

As God unveiled his will to Moses the text quickly intervenes with that proverbial word as only it can. *But...* "Moses said to God, 'Who am I that I should go to Pharaoh...?'" (Exodus 3:11) As we have come to recognize, and more than a few have come to appreciate, Moses' response is classic. Moses' response serves as a precursor to how we respond today. It is as if we are listening to ourselves. "Who, me? Certainly not me, God. Maybe him, but not me. Besides, remember the blessing I received the last time I handled something on your behalf? Forty years of nothing, all for doing what I thought was right. Well, you may have forgotten that, God, but I have not."

Of course, God only very rarely gives into our pleas to the contrary, despite our valiant efforts. He persists. He remains steadfast, "for the gifts and the calling of God are irrevocable." (Romans 11:29) And if we are being honest with ourselves, we often do not like his ways, at all. In fact, some of his ways appear outright unwise, counter to common sense, even ridiculous at times. But, of course, as Dr. J. Vernon McGee inadvertently synthesized my entire attitude regarding God's ways, "This is God's universe, and he does things his way. You may have a better way, but you don't have a universe."

So, come now; let us be reasonable, God said. I am offering you an opportunity. Greatly paraphrased, God is saying to Moses, "I am not asking you to go. I am extending to you a personal invitation. In fact, I am not telling you to go, at least per se, though you are going. I am offering you an opportunity to go. I am offering you an opportunity to fulfill my calling on your life, so come now, and I will send you so that you may bring my people out of bondage. No, it will not be easy. It will be challenging at times and even outright intolerable at others, but ultimately, there is no risk of which I am unaware. I will be with you. Come now, and watch me work," with emphasis on the latter.

Yet Moses attempts to negotiate with God like a defiant child, the defiant child we all become under similar circumstances.

Moses received a personal invitation from God Almighty and resisted. Like most, we may go, but we will only go kicking and screaming. The irony of course is, resist as we might, we will go, or live to wish we had.

Would Moses go? Would Moses yield? Or merely live to wish he had? For years Moses had no doubt longed to be in God's graces again. Some forty years had now passed since killing the Egyptian. Forty years of pondering, forty years of frustration, of struggling, of longing to understand God's ways, and a lifetime of accepting his ways.

To borrow from the Christian musical talent of Big Daddy Weave, *the only name that mattered*[6] to Moses; would he accept that name? The name who had long forgiven him. Would that name matter? The name who had provided for him when he could no longer provide for himself. The name who had comforted him when comfort was not found. The name who had quietly walked alongside him, when he thought he walked alone. The name Moses needed most, the only name that mattered, he resisted.

---

[6] Big Daddy Weave. The only name that matters to me. Love come to life: The Redeemed Edition. World Label Group.

Only after the anger of God became evident does Moses yield. Note however, that during Moses' deliberation, God revealed how liberation of his people would occur. He even demonstrated his powers through wonders that magicians would later attempt to replicate. Nonetheless, Moses hesitated. He resisted. But, "What if they will not believe me...?" (Exodus 4:1) And, when moping and questioning did not work, Moses resorted to begging. "Please, Lord, I have never been eloquent... I am slow of speech and slow of tongue." (Exodus 4:10) "Yes, someone should go indeed, Lord, just not me." Despite getting nowhere, Moses continues to beg. Out of desperation, he formally pleads. "Please, Lord, send the message with whomever you want, just not me." (*cf.* Exodus 4:13)

Herein lies a fundamental problem. God never calls someone else to do what he has called you to do. Nor does he defer when you defiantly refuse. He does not pout, nor panic; he waits. Sometimes he waits patiently and sometimes he waits not so patiently, increasing the pressure with each passing day. Such was the case here with Moses. He called Moses, and as for many reading these words, it is you. It is you he has called. Read that again; it is you he has called, friend. He has extended a personal invitation to you, and with that invitation he has extended an opportunity for you to know God as only few will know him. And he waits.

No, he may not be calling you to the foreign mission field to serve in some Godless shell of a makeshift country; it may be something simple that you have resisted for years. Maybe to merely speak to a neighbor, or maybe just to forgive. But of this, you can be certain; if we truly sought his will for our lives, and obeyed by following, the world would rotate on its axis. Lives would be radically altered as our priorities changed.

Through much hesitation, Moses accepts God's call, and just as he was coming to terms with accepting God's call to deliver his people from bondage, calamity hits. So like God. Moses is hit on his blindside, something that runs counter to what most Christians seem to believe; just follow God and life will be peachy. If this were the case, Moses would have readily followed God, but remember, Moses had spent the last forty years pondering the ways of God. Moses was no dummy. He was no novice at serving God. He had experienced God's capabilities firsthand.

As Moses reluctantly packed his belongings and left with his family for confrontation with Pharaoh, God intervened again, this time to set a few things straight before Moses arrived, to deal directly with something Moses had negated to do. Of course, the timing of this encounter is rather unfortunate for Moses. Just a day or two ago he had yielded to God's call. Before, he was a herder, a field hand, a flunky; and perhaps while not content with that, he had accepted life, such as it was.

Moses had discussed the call with Jethro and his family and packed their belongings, all to undertake a trip with minimal information. At this point, Moses only knew that he and the elders of Egypt were to confront a ruthless dictator known for exerting wickedness on God's people, with a stick and what most would consider a couple of magic tricks.

As time would soon tell, however, God was serious, deadly serious. The encounter with God that night was not haphazardly planned. It was not as if while thinking about Moses' departure that God remembered, "Oh yea, Moses, one more thing before you go." No, as with the previous encounter this meeting would be orchestrated directly by God—and so would the timing. God backed Moses into an awkward position, exactly where he wanted him. And there, he would deal with him.

Following eighty years of preparation, Moses had not only yielded to God's will, he was now fulfilling God's will. When Moses was most vulnerable, just as he was beginning his journey, God confronted him again, and he minced no words. He confronted him for one reason—to kill him,[7] to kill him for negating to fulfill his instructions regarding circumcision. Had Zipporah not immediately intervened, of course, and circumcised their son on Moses' behalf, God would have surely put Moses to death for his sin. As such, Moses learned quickly God's position regarding disobedience, as if the past forty years were not enough. Just as Moses thought God had overlooked it, he addressed it with vengeance. Moses learned quickly that he was not merely taking a trip; he was enduring a journey, a journey that would require total obedience the balance of his life, as he exchanged his will for *His* will.

An investigation into Moses' calling would be incomplete, however, without at least a cursory review regarding when he was called. After being born into the house of Levi, Moses is taken in

---

[7] Though not within the scope of this discussion, certainly I am not the only person ever to ponder this dilemma. God called Moses, and immediately sought to destroy him. Purging Moses' past sin, I can accept, but intent on killing him as a result of this sin requires much deeper consideration, perhaps such consideration that I, myself, cannot render.

by the daughter of Pharaoh, where he would have the best life has to offer. For the first forty years of his life, he would receive the finest of everything. Albeit unknown to most, he would be a Hebrew destined for a life of oppression now living in the luxuries of the Egyptian kingdom. He would eat the finest foods, have the finest friends, have the finest clothes, and earn the finest education. He would never lack. He would be exposed to fortune and fame. Moreover, he would have fortune and fame. Indeed, he was destined for greatness, at least for now.

God had other plans for Moses, however. At the age of forty, upon seeing an Egyptian beating his fellow Hebrew, Moses struck the Egyptian and buried his body in the sand. "No worries, God. I will take care of the Egyptian for you." And perhaps just as Moses thought his deed was an act of love for God's people, his fellow Hebrews turned on him, calling him out for the murder. As Moses attempted to dissolve a fight between the two Hebrews, one of them summed up their attitudes toward the powerful with two pointed questions. "Who made you a prince or judge over us? Are you intending to kill me, as you killed the Egyptian?" (Exodus 2:14) Moses' so-called act of love for God's people was revealed by the very people he sought to protect.

Ironically, Moses' outburst the previous day would serve as a precursor to events that would later unfold in his life. In taking matters into his own hands, arguably, Moses moved more quickly against the corruption inflicted upon the Israelites by the Egyptians than God planned, though by this time God's people had been in bondage for more than four centuries. So perhaps such is understandable on Moses' part when we thoroughly understand the situation. Waiting on God is most often analogous to watching red paint absorb into new drywall, where the more you paint, the more you paint.

But let's put this situation in a modern-day perspective, lest we be too hard on Joseph. During the seven years of famine foretold in Genesis 41, Egypt took the first steps toward becoming a socialist country, and eventually, one ruled by a tyrannical government. The shift from capitalism to socialism occurred when the Israelites and presumably many Egyptians, sold out to the government under Joseph's leadership as they exchanged their horses, donkeys, livestock, and flocks—and themselves—for food. They became slaves, something that would return to haunt them repeatedly with Joseph's passing, for some 157,000 days (430 years). Resulting from their decision to sell out to the government, government taskmasters ruled over them, beating them into submission, beating them into performing work for Pharaoh and his government employees, very, very similarly to what we now see in the United States, where a decreasing few work on behalf of government employees and those too sorry to work. Read the book of Exodus to note the striking similarities between Israel selling out to the government and the US selling out to the government. The parallels are so much so that the socio-political and socio-economic aspects of Egypt and the United States look very similar to countries under, or rapidly headed for, complete tyranny, where We the People, i.e. private-sector citizens, is beaten into submission by the very government employees we feed, e.g. taskmasters, police, judicial employees, agencies of various and every form, and the like. They—government employees and others we feed—control us, as they did God's people, and they control us because, like the Israelites, we slowly allow them, until we are but "sheeple" doing as we are ordered by out-of-control, under-achieving, unaccountable government employees at every level—local, state, and federal. Perhaps it is far time government employees made their own "bricks."

As a Hebrew, Moses had surely tired of standing idly by as his fellow Israelites were beaten into providing for those too sorry to make their own bricks. Call it like it is, friend. He had tired of the control Pharaoh and his team of evil misfits wielded over God's people. The situation was, sadly, analogous to what we now have from government employees in the United States today; complete authority, total autonomy, and zero accountability. Government control. Tyranny. The parallels are startling. As Egyptian leaders came and went, Egypt became a dictatorship ruled by evil men who had no fear of God. Such is always the case with unbridled power. And as was the case with God's people, there will be no change in the US until God intervenes to take us to the Promised Land. Until then, I can only tell you:

> *There is a blood that cost a life*
> *Paid my way, death its price*
> *When it flowed down from the cross*
> *My sins were gone, my sins forgot*
> *There is a grave tried to hide*
> *This precious blood that gave me life*
> *In three days, He breathed again*
> *Rose to stand in my defense*
> *So, I come to tell you. He's alive.*[8]

Moses stood in the face of adversity that day. He stood in the face of Pharaoh. Moses understood right from wrong. He knew where the line in the sand was drawn, as opposed to what we

---

[8] Springer, R. & Wooten, P. (2011). This Blood. Integrity Music.

have in America today, where truth and *the Truth* are subjective to its beholder. He stood against these dark forces, though he obviously feared the repercussions of his actions from the government, as he hid the Egyptian's body after killing him.

Such fear was warranted; he had watched tyranny in his government play out for forty years up close and personal. He had witnessed the beatings. The enslavement. The stealing from those who worked by those who did not. The harsh reality God's people lived day in and day out.

Nonetheless, be reminded that Moses personally benefited from the oppression of God's people, so he was not exactly innocent here. He was housed at the expense of others. He ate at the expense of others. He enjoyed life at the expense of others. His mere existence was at the expense of others, but apparently the unwarranted taking had become despicable to him. The reality his brothers and sisters endured eventually got to him, and he despised such ill-gotten gain. It made him sick. I just wish it made more people in America sick than me, as God is very, very clear regarding this topic; "...if anyone is not willing to work, then he is not to eat, either." (2 Thessalonians 3:10)

Despite his intention of protecting one of God's children from an evil Egyptian,[9] Moses' life would turn for the worse. Forced to flee the life of royalty he had come to expect, he would now spend the next forty years wondering aimlessly in the deserts of Midian,[10] essentially working as a field hand for his father in law, Jethro.

Now he would be *just* Moses. Fortune and fame would no longer realistically be part of his thought processes. Eventually perhaps, fortune and fame would leave his thoughts altogether. Their memories would become so distant it would seem they never existed, but certainly never to the point that Moses would no longer be haunted by this unfortunate turn of events. His lack of any foreseeable successes would now be, as Paul stated, a thorn in his flesh (*cf.* 2 Corinthians 12). Always there, taunting him. Never leaving, even for a moment, and never yielding. Oh, the heart may remain steadfast, but the flesh would struggle.

---

[9] The Egyptian was almost certainly one of the taskmasters God referred to in Exodus 3. Taskmasters were the equivalent of corrupt police today, and they were infamous for controlling people. Taskmasters worked for Pharaoh's government, beating people into submission so they could have that which they did not earn; this is nearly identical to what we see in government today. For additional reading, refer to a previous book I wrote on this subject: Fall of a Nation: A Biblical Perspective of a Modern Problem, 2012, Westbow Press / Thomas Nelson Publishing, Indiana.
[10] The Midian area lies within the countries of Israel and Saudi Arabia.

Moses would become a washed-up has-been, but the process of becoming a washed-up has-been is not a position someone just assumes, or acquires. The position is not given to you. You do not walk in and assume the responsibilities and rights thereof; quite the contrary. The position is earned; it is never an entitlement. One must labor long and hard to acquire the esteem brought about by being a washed-up has-been. And the thorn of never amounting to anything but an outcast, of never above being a low life, would haunt him, again. And again.

For the next forty years, Moses would scratch out a life working for his father-in-law, a man who was priest of Midian before ironically becoming an outcast himself. Moses had everything. Now he had nothing. How degrading. How humiliating. He was no longer served; he was the servant. He tended the flocks. Yesterday, today, tomorrow, and the day after tomorrow, he would be but a shepherd. On and on his days would go caring for the animals, alone only with his thoughts for company. His life no longer had a sense of purpose. No goals, no objectives, and no hope. Hope had long given way to accepted despair. No short eight-hour workdays with promising colleagues for Moses. No two-hour lunches to discuss activities of the approaching weekend with friends. Long hours, very long hours.

Perhaps eighteen or twenty-hour days were the rule rather than the exception. Likely, first to rise, last to lie. Exhausted, day after day, he toiled for forty arduous years, nearly 15,000 days in the sweltering heat and freezing cold alone with his thoughts. No purpose.

Then God showed up.

Herbert M Barber, Jr, PhD, PhD

The Perception of Blessing

Blessing is an oddity, of sorts. It is something we seem only to understand in the context of how we view good. It somehow goes against the grain to view the trials and struggles we endue as anything other than negative.

The same holds true for Christian and non-Christian. We feel blessed when life is good. We have a great spouse. Our kids do well in school, or they are grown with great kids of their own. We have strong ties with our family and church. We have a great job, nice home, and two cars. We have great friends, and even a pet or two. Life is good. We are blessed.

Many persons have such lives. Jesus, himself, had such a life. Perhaps we could say that he was living every Jew's dream. He came from a nice family with God-fearing parents. He had a nice home, spent time in the temple, and was successful in the family business. He was blessed.

Isaac was blessed. From his labors, he reaped one hundred-fold. As the text states, he "continued to grow richer until he became very wealthy." (Genesis 26:13) Similarly, Solomon was blessed. He became "greater than all the kings of the earth in riches and wisdom." (2 Chronicles 9:9)

To appreciate blessing fully, however, we must first understand its older sister, wisdom. Wisdom never occurs without understanding, and neither come without a cost, and in many cases, a substantial cost; but as the writer of Ecclesiastes noted, wisdom is better than folly. (3:10)

Job learned this lesson. He learned it the hard way, for there is no other way. Job had seven sons and three daughters. He owned 7,000 sheep, 3,000 camels, 500 yokes of oxen, 500 female donkeys, and he had several servants. Job was "the greatest of all the men of the east." (Job 1:3)

By any standard, Job was blessed. Few persons of his day knew such blessings. Even by today's standards, Job was wealthy. All that life offered was at his disposal. He never wondered whether his daily needs would be met—or whether his children would have food to eat or a place to lay their heads. He never stayed home because he could not afford food to fuel his camels or the supplies his donkeys would carry during his travels. Given every measure, Job had the best that life had to offer. Moreover, we find in Job 1:1 and 1:8 that Job was "blameless," meaning not that he was without sin but rather, that Job recognized God's sovereignty, yielded to such, and therefore, was complete.[11]

Nonetheless, if we look closely, it appears that both Satan *and* God set out to destroy Job and life as he knew it. Pay particular attention to the first chapter of Job. Satan and God negotiate Job's demise. However, note that Satan does not beg God to allow him to destroy Job; not at all. In fact, God himself offers Job up to Satan! "Have you considered my servant Job?" (Genesis 1:8) In the end, only Job's life is spared. All else is taken, destroyed, or rendered useless.

Job's first report of bad news came when one of his servants reported that his oxen and donkeys had been stolen. Simultaneously, the thieves also killed several of Job's servants. As the servant is still speaking to Job, however, another servant

---

[11] There are several arguments regarding the use of the word "blameless," as used in the Book of Job. The definition as used herein appears to be the most frequently used of all definitions.

rushes in to tell Job that fire has reigned down from the sky and killed other servants, along with his sheep. As if Job's day is not bad enough already, yet another servant rushes in to tell Job of even more servants being killed; and that Job's camels have been stolen, as well. Job then learns that his children were killed in a violent storm (*cf.* Job 1:13-19). And this is only the first day of Job's hell on earth.

Unfortunately, we overlook the details associated with that first day, but consider its gruesome reality. Job had 7,000 sheep. Now he had none. Grazing yesterday; dead today. Camels, oxen and donkeys? All stolen. Here yesterday; gone today. His children and servants? Playing, laughing, and working this morning. Dead this afternoon. Gone. No more.

Place yourself in the events of that day. Forget about the emotional anguish a minute, for most of us could not begin to manage that, so let us not pretend we could. Look at the place physically. Blood and guts strung and strewed across the landscape. Dead animals strewn everywhere as they began to rot in the heat of midday, perhaps for weeks. Vultures everywhere, eating the dead animals. Other scavengers fighting over the carcasses, as if food was limited. Dead children being brought in as time passed; and let us not forget the dead servants who were apparently struck by lightning. They had families, as well. Slaves they may have been, but they were husbands, wives, and children. They too had lives. They too were God's children. They lived every day to the fullest extent possible, and now, they were no more.

Surely, a good God would not inflict even more harm upon his faithful servant, would he? After all, Job was *blameless*. Nonetheless, in a single day Job lost his oxen, donkeys, sheep, camels, most of his servants, and his children. He was living hell on earth, and *he had no control whatsoever over it*. *None*. All that remained were blood and guts coupled with deep, deep anguish, an anguish that he eventually may manage but that he would never overcome. Yet Satan then destroys Job's health. He smites Job "with sore boils from the sole of his foot to the crown of his head," (Job 2:7) because after all, when some is good, more is better. And all the while, God just sat there. Hell had rained down on the one he called blameless, and he just watched it unfold.

So, do you still refer to Job as blessed? Doubtful.

Noah was also blessed. He "found favor in the eyes of the Lord." (Genesis 6:8) Similar to Job, Noah was "a righteous man, blameless." (Genesis 6:9) However, the "earth was filled with violence," (Genesis 6:11) so God set out to destroy man, to blot humankind from the earth, choosing only to save Noah, his family, and a few animals.

Noah was blessed indeed. He walked with God, but he also suffered, a point we often conveniently overlook when considering his life. Look at the days of Noah. Our generation holistically has never witnessed such evil, though we are approaching such similarities given the rate at which evil in our world, at home and abroad, is increasing.

Consider Genesis 6:4. Fallen angels (sons of God) procreated with human beings, creating beings of darkness analogous in stature to beings noted in Greek mythology—part human and part angelic. Of course, most pulpiteers kindly refer to these beings as giants, and in a few more years, pulpiteers will refer to these forces of darkness simply as "gentle giants," if mentioned at all, apparently choosing to disregard that which we cannot accept; or choosing to believe otherwise due to the wicked grotesqueness of such raw evil. Nonetheless, "The Lord was sorry that He had made man on the earth, and He was grieved in His heart." (Genesis 6:6)

Despite this raw evil, or rather due to the evil, Noah and his family labored purposefully as they constructed the ark. But on their best day, they looked like fools. No doubt, they quickly became the laughing stock of the known world. We can imagine that word of some foolish old man and his family building an ark in a region where rain had become a distant memory spread quickly. Word traveled like wild fire, much as gossip does in our day—and the juicier the gossip, the faster it spreads. People must have journeyed long distances to see the foolishness of this old man called Noah. "Hey, did you hear about the old man building that big boat in the middle of nowhere? Yea; says it's gonna flood."

Almost certainly, Job was building the ark under great duress. Not only was he building a massive boat, he had no idea whether it would float—or that it would actually rain. Besides, Archimedes, that great mathematician credited with deriving the engineering equations to leverage buoyant forces in overcoming the sinking effects of objects on water, had yet to be born. More importantly however, Moses was building the ark under extreme circumstances predicated upon a corrupted and evil society, one filled with demonic activity, mass killings, illicit sexual acts, and other forms of vulgarity. But as ridiculous as he must have appeared, Noah was following the will of God.

But at least to me, all of this begs the question, "What was God doing while this darkness fell across his earth?" While heaven's angels were falling from heaven to procreate with women? What was he doing while such grotesque evil played out? He was watching it happen; that's what he was doing. Watching it happen, just as he is doing in our day, today. At least for now. But be reminded, there will come a day when he will do more than watch.

Until then, Noah moved forward with God's will, remembering that this was not his will; it was God's vision. His job was merely to see the vision through fulfillment. As Richard Blackaby notes regarding spiritual leadership, "The problem with Christian leaders is not that they don't know what God wants them to do. They problem is …. they are unwilling to do it." Our friend Noah knew what God called him to do, and he was doing it. Regardless the foolishness of it all, regardless the darkness surrounding the call, he was doing it. And mind you, no, he wasn't living the dream; he was fulling God's vision.

Indeed, Noah was anomalous for his day, but how could the average person not think of Noah and his team of misfits as fools? For starters, he obviously feared God and respected his authority, both contrary to others on earth during this wicked period in time and today. To top it off, he was building a boat that would end up being 450ft long by 75ft wide by 45ft high.[12] For the mathematically challenged, that is one and a half times longer than a football field, a little less than the width of the same field, and about half as tall as the average pine tree in the South. As such, constructing a large boat in those days had to require years of effort that were no doubt made longer with the scorching ridicule Noah endured.[13] By secular standards, Noah looked like a mad man, and for all practical purposes, he was a fool.

Even after Noah was proven not to be the fool society found him to be—the day it began raining—what did it matter at that point? It was not as if Job could say, "I told you so." There was no one left to tell. I don't know; maybe he ran upstairs, slammed the

---

[12] If you are following this story in the text, be aware that one cubit is approximately 1.5 feet, or .46 meters.

[13] Construction of the ark likely required less than 100 years. Noah became father of Shem, Ham, and Japheth when he was approximately 500 years old (Genesis 5:32), and the flood occurred when Noah was 600 years old (Genesis 7:6). Further, Noah died at 950 years of age (Genesis 9:29).

door, stuck his head out the window, and yelled, "I told you so! I told you so, you big dummy! Who's the mad man now?" I would have, but I seriously doubt he did.

So Noah's life was spared, but now what would he do? Where was he going? Nowhere. He would float on his homemade raft, aimlessly floating with no direction and no destination. Certainly, the water there was similar to the water here. Nothing else to see; blue water here, blue water there. While being grateful for having his life spared, now he now had no goal and no direction. At least while he was building the boat, he had a decent objective. Now he was in control of absolutely nothing. Not a thing. Now he had no choice but to trust God.

Perhaps worse, his living arrangements and responsibilities now must have been seen as less than preferable after the first few days of novelty subsided. We can imagine his situation as quite dismal. Dead people and animals floating by the thousands. Noah himself floated aimlessly on a makeshift boat with no end in sight. He had no real goals and no serious objectives. No seemingly worthwhile purpose. Limited food, even less rest, and mindless work that had no end. He may have even been seasick. Day after day, his days would be filled with miserable living conditions, to the point that we would consider them intolerable today. Could you imagine living with hundreds of stinking animals day after day, up close and personal?

Such is the case with any difficult call God places on your life, especially those that involve serving other people. Oh, he was blessed, alright. But up close and personal, his call and its subsequent blessings was messy. Like Noah, behind the glitz and glamour, behind the scenes, what you endured to get here, and what you endure daily to remain, is nasty. Often times, it is humiliating, degrading, and about as far away from the glitz and glamour witnessed by outsiders as possible. Oh, you see me smile, you may hear me laugh, and you may be encouraged by my words, but may you never have the displeasure of knowing what it took to get here, for fully understanding such would shake your spiritual foundation to its core.

The problem with blessing is not that we do not welcome it with open arms, it is that we do not understand blessing, what it is, let alone how it is received. Our understanding of blessing is based upon flawed constructs derived through a flawed paradigm, which I personally believe resulted through erroneous messages from modern day teachings. As we say in statistics, *trash in, trash out.* We primarily only perceive blessing in the context of good, as something positive, and thus, we have a skewed definition entirely. It is only when we use another lens altogether that we begin to gain insight into how God defines blessing, and a shift occurs in a flawed and destructive paradigm that has made its way into America's churches the last few decades.

Like Noah, Job was blessed. He had arrived. He had everything a man could want from life. His was blessed indeed, but moreover, he realized from whom those blessings came. However, just when God's blessings seemed to have no end, Job was destroyed, and life became unrecognizable. In a single day, he became a fragment of the man he was. Now he was unrecognizable. However, even after losing everything and becoming essentially nonexistent from a human perspective, Job's anguish was only beginning. The initial shock and awe was over, thank God, but the fallout would remain.

And like Job, Noah was righteous. How could one argue to the contrary? Of the world's population, God spared only his family from certain death. However, life as Noah knew it had certainly changed. He no longer went about his day simply serving

God and meeting the needs of his family. He no longer enjoyed the pleasures of life. No, he now spent his days shoveling manure. Day in and day out, he and his family sweated out their days in the filth and stench of an enclosed homemade dungeon filled with stinking animals as they drifted aimlessly across open waters. In the end, Noah would survive the storm, but now what? In all fairness to Noah and his steadfast relationship with his maker, he had no idea. Until God moved and rescinded the water, he would float with no direction whatsoever, there with his family, with his only goal for every day being to shovel animal waste from this corner of the room to the other.

When God calls, life is like that. The interlude between destruction and understanding, the fallout, is more painful than the destruction itself. In many cases, we merely thought the destruction was bad. The fallout is often worse, much worse. Destruction comes and goes. Fallout endures; fallout lingers. It hangs around, and if we are not very careful, it moves into our homes permanently and becomes who we are. It then defines us.

The stock market crashes and you lose what has taken a lifetime to build. A child is taken home after years of struggle to keep him alive. Your marriage of 25 years abruptly ends, or your spouse of 50 years is taken home. The pregnancy you so desperately sought for more than a decade only ends in miscarriage, again. Your best friend and business partner swindles you out of millions of dollars on a deal you spent years developing. Or, the test results you have dreaded return positive, and all second opinions have been exhausted. Yet somehow, we are expected to somehow see blessing.

Joseph was thrown in the pit in a matter of seconds. His life was destroyed in a few quick minutes, and it all happened with a purpose driven by darkness. It was direct and swift. Yet the fallout endures. It is present tense. It goes nowhere. It sets with baited breath to destroy the last remaining hope you have in humanity and God, himself. It remains behind to torture you, to drive your loss home, to ensure that each passing day is not without ambiguity, pain, and suffering to ensure that each passing day is, well, your normal.

When you are at work, fallout sits in the chair beside you. When you go away for a weekend getaway to recover, it packs a bag to enjoy the trip with you. You wrestle with fallout day and night. Joseph did. Why did my own brothers betray me? How could they? We are family. Joseph would ponder it once a day, all day. It is all he would consider—until it becomes your life. Perhaps you too have been there, so you know; if you are not very, very careful, fallout becomes you, who you are, and you begin to smell like it. Your days are long, and your nights are longer.

You lie awake at night as you consider the fiery trial that initially strengthened your marriage that now tears it apart. How could you not? Fallout now sleeps between you and your spouse, at least until you are nudged out altogether.

You toss and turn without rest as you contemplate whether your business can handle the millions of dollars in receivables that will never come due in whole to the ill intent of one you considered your lifelong friend. You toss. You turn. Or years later you still wrestle with false accusations that destroyed your very being, then and now. The anger still lies just beneath the surface, poised to explode at a moment's notice; and again you loathe. You despise. Yet somehow, you are supposed to smile while being forced to turn lemons into lemonade. Besides, lest you allow fallout to completely destroy you, you have but that single choice—to make lemonade.

As with Job, your friends are of little value, assuming you have any friends left. They do not understand the pain, *your* pain; their lives remain intact. Their struggles are but trivial to you. After all, who really cares that they had to work late yesterday and were unable to get the brownies to school on time, that they had to replace the transmission in their car, or that their child stayed out past curfew? Their insight is merely an endless supply of useless infinite wisdom. How could they understand your pain? You do not understand your pain, and on many occasions, you are not certain even God understands your pain. Even so, you are too angry to understand your pain. Perhaps you do not care to understand your pain. You just want it to go away—with those responsible with it, and if that includes God, perhaps him too.

And for some reason those watered-down self-help sermons coming from your church's pulpit on Sundays no longer matter. No substance. No depth. Just plain shallow. You could walk across their depths like Peter walked across water—without sinking. Besides, one who has been deeply hurt by God, or his instruments, has no interest in hearing watered down versions regarding how to be happy. Such pathetic messages are ridiculous and suited only for novice Christians who have never battled God's definitive call for one to deny self completely, despite having minimal information as to how the cause associated with the call will ever be realized, let alone God's vision.

Nonetheless, it is during these intervals, these periods between destruction and understanding, which are the most significant times in our lives, for it is during these painful intervals that God prepares us for greatness, for significance. It is during the fallout associated with these trials that he prepares us to fulfill his vision *with* our lives. So, if it is possible for God to waiver in his attentiveness toward us, it is not during these intervals; no, to the contrary, it is during these painful intervals of immense suffering that he provides his utmost attention. Personal attention. Oh, he is there. He is right there with you. You may not feel his presence. In fact, you may not want him there, but he is there nevertheless. On many, many occasions he is not only there, he is the one inflicting the pain, not Satan, as most Christians would have you believe. So, your turmoil continues despite your pleas to the contrary.

Despite our turmoil, however, it is during our weakest times when God does his greatest work in us, as his greatest work only comes through complete denial of self. As A.W. Tozer so eloquently surmised, "It is doubtful whether God can use a man greatly, until first He wounds him deeply." So where is the true blessing? Where does it lie? Is it found during the harvest? Not really. It is found during the planting, during the droughts in our life.

Briefly consider Abraham. His walk to sacrifice his son was arguably the most painful experience of his life. The walk was horrific. It had to be, for he too was human. He was *only* human. He took his loving son on a hiking expedition—following God's will, mind you—to sacrifice his son. "Take now your son, your only son, whom you love, Isaac, and go to the land of Moriah, and offer him there as a burnt offering..." (Genesis 22:2) So Abraham packed all he needed for the trip, except the sacrificial animal, but unknown to his son, that too had been packed. However, Abraham endured the walk. So did Job and Noah. All three endured their own walks of immense pain and suffering. Many of us do, but for a select few, the suffering is far greater than most, far greater. And it is these people God uses to set the world on fire for his benefit.

Like Job and these other men, few people know suffering better than Joseph. Subsequently, few people understand blessing better than Joseph.

While Joseph had likely slept a little late that morning, his older brothers had long been up, preparing to tend the family business of herding animals. As they prepared, they paused just long enough to listen to their baby brother's latest dream of lording over them, as if he was their moral superior, or perhaps worse, they were his personal servants. To the contrary, however, they had no use for Joseph, for he was spoiled. However, he was the favored son, and being the favored son did not come without privileges. You are allowed to sleep a little later than your siblings, hang around the house a little longer, work a little less, and play a little more. You even get to wear name-brand clothes; you know the kind, those top-shelf-kind that are flamboyant, those with the horse logo, or another distinguishing feature that screams, I am better than you. Life is just better when you are the baby of the family.

What was most likely several days after Joseph's brothers had left Hebron to pasture their flocks in Shechem,[14] Joseph's father Israel sends him to check on the welfare of his older

---

[14] Joseph's family lived in Hebron, a city in the West Bank, so the trip to Shechem most likely put his brothers traveling through Bethlehem and Jerusalem, cities north of Hebron. The distance between Hebron and Shechem is approximately 50-60 miles, or 80-96km.

brothers. "Go now and see about the welfare of your brothers and the welfare of the flock; and bring word back to me." (Genesis 37:18) By this time, however, his brothers were longing for the comforts of home, as their journey had taken them some 50 miles. Likewise, Joseph's journey to check on their well-being would be long, tiresome, and arduous. Nonetheless, he set out, following the will of his father.

Only retrospectively do we learn that God had called Joseph to fulfill a very specific purpose in life, one he could not fulfill from the comfort of his father's house where he could be pampered as the baby in the family. God had appointed Joseph to follow a specific path, a path that would lead him through many, many difficult trials in life. And that first pit, the one his brothers tossed him in; that pit would come along with him, for his trials would take him to the brink of disaster on countless occasions. And it would all stem from one small act of obedience on Joseph's part, coupled with one small act of disobedience on the part of others.

Before his life would end, Joseph's preparation for his eventual role as leader would lead him down a path traveled by few and envied by none. His path would be difficult on the good days. There would be loneliness. There would be isolation. There would be uncertainty. There would be pain, and there would be suffering; pain and immense suffering that only few experience.

The average Christian today would never seek such a path, as most Christians are satisfied with a status quo relationship with Christ. Just answer my occasional prayer, God; I will attend church on Sundays and all will be well. Ho-hum. God is good. We know this to be true, though we certainly would never admit it. It is easily recognizable in most Christians on Sunday morning. Unfortunately, this type relationship with Christ appears to be more the rule today than the exception. Worse, most people today have no relationship with Christ at all, opting rather to place their eternity in their own hands. In fact, as I previously estimated in an earlier book, consider what occurs as you listen to your next sermon.

By my count, the population of self-proclaimed Christians in the world is around 27.7 percent of the world's population of seven billion. This is after deducting the populations of religions that claim to be Christian but are not, such as Mormons and Jehovah Witnesses. This places the number of unsaved in this world at a whopping 5.1 billion people (72.3%). If the number of people who die in the world every year is approximately 56.9 million people, and 72.3 percent are unsaved, roughly 41 million people (specifically, 40,884,480 persons) go to hell every year. That's 786,240 people a week! Breaking these numbers down further, approximately 78 people in the world go to hell every single minute of every single day of the week, month after month, and year after year. Worse, this rate is increasing as the world's population increases, and even outpacing that growth rate, given the booming non-believing populations of Muslims and others. Therefore, during the average 25-minute sermon, while we are all listening to jokes and watered down secular self-help sermons, approximately 1,950 people enter the gates of hell. Consider the reality of this; by the end of every sermon you hear, day or night, almost 2,000 people have experienced the flames of hell—and the wrath of God![15]

---

[15] Barber, H. (2012). Fall of a Nation: A biblical perspective on a modern problem. Westbow Press/Thomas Nelson. Indianapolis.

Even for these foolish souls destined for eternity in hell, we all want success in life. We all want to be blessed, but honestly, the methods we use to "earn" blessing, to acquire significance, could not run more counter to the ways of God.

Years ago, when I began my studies for my first doctorate, someone said to me, "I can't believe you are earning your Ph.D. That will take forever! You're going to be 35 when you finally finish!" Not to be outwitted, I responded, "Well, how old will I be when I get to be 35 and I did not earn a Ph.D.?"

Of course, my position regarding all *talk* and little *do* has always been, "If you didn't bother to show up for spring practice, don't expect to play in the Super Bowl." Perhaps a weak analogy given the serious nature of the topic herein, but it reminds me of the mountains of proud pastors referring to themselves as doctor so-and-so who have never earned a real doctorate (PhD). Humor me as I acknowledge their circumvented paths to the Super Bowl, and as I discuss one of the greatest lies we see in many pastors and others today.

The highest academic degree awarded in the United States and nearly every other country is the Doctor of Philosophy (PhD), an academic degree most notably granted following completion of a bachelor's degree and master's degree, followed by preliminary testing, doctoral coursework, significant oral and written testing, creation of new knowledge in a given body of literature via scientific research, and defense of that research against the scientific scrutiny of other doctors. Thus, the title "Doctor" is only awarded after successfully earning years of academic education and individually conducting independent scientific research—not after completing a few years of training.

Allow me to explain further. In every country in the world, including the United States, "Doctor" is a title, not a profession, nor a vocation. Academically, professionally, and otherwise, a PhD recipient (and research-based EdD and ThD recipient) is the only holder of what is considered a doctoral degree. All other so-called "doctorate" degrees, such as the MD, DO, OD, DMD, DDS, DMin, JD, and others, are considered professional degrees, many that do not require even the most basic degree, a four-year bachelor's degree, let alone a rigorous master's degree, advanced doctoral coursework, and the completion of original scientific research. For example, an MD degree in the top medical schools in this country, such as Harvard and Emory, do not require admitting nor graduating students to have earned a bachelor's degree prior to admissions, nor prior to graduation. The applicant must merely complete eight to ten courses in the basic sciences, such as chemistry, biology, anatomy, physiology, and similar courses, courses most undergraduates complete within their normal course of study toward their bachelor's degree. After completing approximately two years of education at the undergraduate level and two years of medical training, they then complete additional training, up to say, three to ten years. They are, in fact, well trained. However, training should not be confused with *education*. And here lies the difference between a doctoral degree and a professional degree. Education teaches one to think, to reason, to critique, and to analyze. Training teaches one to do, to complete specific tasks; hence, the phrase, *medical practice*.

Consider the education of an engineer. An engineer in any discipline must complete three to five calculus courses, differential equations, linear equations and modeling, one to two programming languages, one to two chemistry courses, three calculus-based physics courses, and all the normal core courses every other student takes, prior to beginning their engineering educations. Their engineering educations only get more demanding mathematically, and otherwise, as they then must apply the educations they have acquired to solve complex problems using what we would consider basic mathematics and physics. But this is not the point; following graduation, to serve as a professional engineer, the young engineer must then pass an eight-hour exam covering every engineering course they had in their undergraduate program, a monumental undertaking. Following successful completion of this exam, they then serve four to seven years under a professional engineer, and following this, they then must sit and pass another eight-hour exam. In addition, if they want to serve as, say, a structural engineer, they then must successfully pass a 16-hour exam covering seismic engineering and the like, but such only occurs after serving three additional years under another professional engineer who is also a licensed structural engineer. Of course, while on the course of becoming licensed as a structural engineer, most persons have continued their formal educations, with many earning their master's degrees and doctorates in engineering, as it is nearly impossible to conduct advanced structural engineering without having at least a master's degree. The point is, many fields require training, nearly all—and some even require *education*. Look at it this way; when a physician makes a mistake, one person dies. When a structural engineer makes a mistake, hundreds of persons die. Certainly, both fields are important, but in the end, physicians are trained, not educated. Hence, the reason the US Department of Education does not consider the MD a doctoral degree.

Similarly, though not identical by far, a DMin degree is not a doctoral degree, either, as there is no scientific research component associated with their preparation. That said, the DMin recipient may think their DMin project is scientific research, qualifying them for the academic title of doctor, but let me pose a pointed question: How many times do you see DMin projects published in *refereed* journals, those refereed by doctors, as you would most PhD dissertations and other research papers? Never, and this is no coincidence because these projects are merely ramblings and writings, not research. Thus, their work would never be accepted as scientific research. Besides, how would a DMin ever conduct research when they have not completed multiple courses in advanced research design, research methodology, measurement, statistics, linear and non-linear systems modeling, and many, many other courses in research, particularly in the mathematical sciences?

The DMin is a professional degree, and there is nothing wrong with that. Most DMin recipients must first earn a three-year MDiv degree prior to admissions, along with their earlier bachelor's degree, so without question, some pastors are well educated, and trained. However, the DMin is not considered a doctorate in academic circles. However, if you need further evidence that an MD, DMin, and the like are not doctorates, why does the *National Survey of Earned Doctorates* not track these graduates and their research; you know, the medium through which the United States of America tracks the intellect of the nation's human capital? Because, while certainly they may be an intellectual giant, their degrees are not at the doctoral level.

But the trek toward earning the title doctor, toward playing in the Super Bowl, gets much worse, and it is important, so bear with me. Many, many, many pastors refer to themselves as doctor so and so. That fact is established. But what is also established is the fact that these same pastors have never darkened the door of higher learning at the doctoral level. Consider the worst of the bunch, David Jeremiah. Mr. Jeremiah has never earned a doctoral degree in his life—from any university of higher learning. Yet Mr. Jeremiah blasts the title doctor in front of his name on every book he sells, on his websites, on every bio, and from every pulpit. He is a liar. Nothing else. Honestly, I cannot read his books, nor watch him on television, all because he wakes every day and repeats the same lie, day after day after day. The man doesn't even have a DMin, let alone a doctorate.

But why is this so important? Because it is a matter of character. Lying about his lack of education destroys his ministry. He knows it is a lie, I know it's a lie, and now you know it's a lie; and you can bet God knows it is a lie. Yet, the good "doctor" fools many, many persons with the passing of every day. Not me, however. To me, he is just another person lying in an attempt to cover his lack of education. And of course, it matters because Mr. Jeremiah, like all others claiming to be doctors, are fraudulently benefiting financially from the title as they falsely claim to be something they are not; hence, the move across some states in the US to consider use of the title "Doctor" without having earned a PhD a crime. Yes, a crime, for what else is fraud?

Even so, perhaps we could let Mr. Jeremiah slide with this lie if this same issue was not so rampant in pulpits today. Consider Chuck Swindoll and Ravi Zacharias. Both claim to be doctors; they both use the title, and encourage others use the title; and they are both liars. Neither have earned doctorates. Mr. Swindoll refers to himself as doctor on his church's bio and in a book he co-authored, and he has his friends at Dallas Theological Seminary refer to him as doctor with every introduction—over and over and over. As for Mr. Zacharias, he too refers to himself as doctor on his website, his books, his bios, and from the pulpit—over and over and over. But the man lies about his lack of education; both do. Every day. And when we lie, it makes us *liars*.

Do you need a more complete list of pastors who lie about their educations? Try these on for size: Erwin Lutzer, Creflo Dollar, Fredrick Price, Chuck Missler, James David Manning, Charles Stanley, Jerry Vines, Jerry Falwell, Billy Graham, Joyce Myers, Johnny Hunt, T.D. Jakes, Bill Winston, Stephen Davey, Jack Van Impe, Kenneth Copeland, Mike Murdock, and Rod Parsley—and these are only the well-known pastors who lie about their educations; I have seen hundreds of pastors lie about their educations over the years. Not one of these acclaimed pastors and Bible teachers has an earned doctorate—not one—yet they all refer to themselves as doctor. Their lies tarnish their ministries, and God takes this very seriously; in this case, so much so that these pastors are breaking both the ninth and tenth commandments simultaneously—lying and coveting.

Even the infamous Martin Luther King, or as Eddie Murphy mocked him in the 1988 movie, *Coming to America*, Martin

Luther, *the King*, was not immune from lying when it came to his attempt to play in the Super Bowl. In 1990, Mr. King's academic investigative panel "reluctantly acknowledged... that substantial parts of [Mr.] King's doctoral dissertation and other academic papers from his student years [were] plagiarized." Dr. Clayborne Carson, "a professor of history at Stanford University who was chosen in 1985 by [Mr.] King's widow, Coretta Scott King (who, ironically, also falsely claims to be a doctor)" to investigate these claims of fraud, eventually stated that his team's analysis of "the papers by researchers working on the project had uncovered concepts, sentences and longer passages taken from other sources without attribution throughout [Mr.] King's writings as a theology student" at Boston University.[16] In fact, according to the Martin Luther King Organization itself, "[Mr.] King's dissertation is a result heavily plagiarized. The King Papers Project in 1991 estimated that [at a minimum] 52% of Chapter 2 of the thesis was plagiarized, transcribed from the work of other authors without any indication that the section was an exact reproduction. Looking over the complete annotated version of his thesis, it is clear that in places, page upon successive page is composed of

---

[16] De Palma, A. (1990). Plagiarism seen by scholars in King's Ph.D. dissertation. The New York Times.

concatenated sequences of stolen quotations, with King contributing literally nothing to the text other than by arranging the words of others."[17] In their final report, the review committee stated, "There is no question but that [Mr.] King plagiarized [his] dissertation."[18] Thus, Mr. King was a liar.

Sadly, however, neither the president nor the provost at Boston University had the personal nor academic integrity to revoke the degree from a man who blatantly cheated and lied his way through not only the entire doctoral process, but his entire academic career. Ironically, neither did Dr. John H. Cartwright have the integrity to revoke such deceit, though he served on the investigative panel. Why ironic? Dr. Cartwright not only served on the committee reviewing Mr. King's work, he served as the distinguished professor who holds the Martin Luther King Jr. chair in social ethics at Boston University. And let us never forget, due to his so-called immense contributions to the field of theology, humanity, social justice, and ethics, Mr. King was awarded the Nobel Peace Prize. But again, the man was a liar until his death.

---

[17] King's dissertation (n.d.). Martin Luther King Organization
[18] Gordon, L. (1991). King's doctorate upheld despite plagiarisms. Los Angeles Times.

Indeed, such ill-fated schemes reflect the pathetic state of our entitlement society, a society where even our most prominent pastors would rather lie to their congregations every day than put forth the blood, sweat, and tears that come with earning a doctorate. Sadly, a couple of these pastors noted herein are excellent Biblical expositors, but unfortunately, they expect to play in the Super Bowl while having never spent a single day at spring practice. *Unlike grace, education is earned.* As John MacArthur accurately surmised the Christian walk, they want the Christ without the cross.[19] Sadly, Mr. MacArthur also touts himself as a doctor on the website of the Master's Seminary website, though he never earned a doctoral degree. How unfortunate; Mr. MacArthur is a solid Biblical expositor.

The problem with all *talk* and little *do* is that it typically does not yield meaningful results. For example, college professors with little realistic experience and research in their respective fields are left merely to regurgitate information they, themselves, were taught or read. Such makes for a rather shallow learning experience for the student. As an example, in my first doctoral program an esteemed organizational theory professor rambled

---

[19] MacArthur, J. (2003). Hard to Believe, Thomas Nelson Publishers.

on for several minutes regarding how incorporation of a particular strategy in industry could save corporations millions of dollars. Only after I could take it no further, I stated that we had indeed incorporated this technique on several occasions across multiple platforms, all with no measurable improvement. Of course, this ran counter to his opinion and subsequently earned me a solid B in a course where my grades averaged 96/100. I guess those of us working for Procter & Gamble did not know what we were doing.

Some twenty-five years ago an electrical engineer who was an avid hunter was describing his excitement regarding the prior weekend when he found a large deer in his rifle scope. As the story goes, he details the pounding of his chest and the sweating of his palms as he finally squeezes the trigger to take down the deer. But never one to be outwitted, a structural engineer entered the conversation by responding, "I know! You see this big ole deer standing there, and you get all excited and nervous. You can barely hold your gun still!" Knowing the structural engineer had passed all of the exams to be a certified nerd, the electrical engineer quipped, "What, do you hunt, too?" to which sparky responded, "Well, no, but I've watched it on television."

You know, sometimes you just have to do a little more than watch life on television. Joseph too, would soon learn that lesson. For the chosen, there is always more to life than watching it from afar.

As Joseph packed for his trip to check on his brothers that morning, following his father's will that day would become a pivotal point in his life, one that would serve as the catalyst for a period in his life that he would no doubt ponder again and again. Joseph would indeed do more than watch life from the comforts of afar. He would do much more than that. His faith would not be something he wore on his shirtsleeve, only to be exercised when times became tough. Oh, he would be blessed, but would he view his adversity as blessing, because his life would give new meaning to the term *adversity*?

For eighteen years, Joseph had lived a life of leisure. Perhaps he had indeed worked hard with his brothers from time to time; and at other times, perhaps not. Regardless, he certainly experienced the blessings of life, at least eighteen years' worth. Every day forward, however, would be a challenge for Joseph, a challenge unlike he had ever witnessed, let alone experienced. Pain and suffering would become a way of life. It would become his life. Not yours; *his*. And it would be personal. In fact, every day of his life would present challenges most of us cannot imagine, let alone handle. He would not read how damp and stagnant a waterless pit could be. How hot, nor how cold. He would not grasp the meaning of loneliness by watching a television show, or reading a book. Nor would he come to understand desperation by listening to the discussions of others. He would live it. He would become a lowly slave. Not just a misfit, but a nobody. He would sit in a filthy damp prison for years for something he did not do. He would suffer repeatedly for doing right, all for following his father's will. However, from 18 on, Joseph's life would paint a picture of committed faithfulness and obedience despite a life filled with insurmountable human challenges, challenges that no sane person would envy.

On that day, that proverbial day that would eventually lead him to an enviable life with God, Joseph approached his brothers. He was there to check on their welfare; and they were there to destroy his.

"Here comes this dreamer!" (Genesis 37:19) Not just any dreamer, *this* dreamer, the one person who gets under our skin more than any other. The one who thinks he is special. The pampered brat in his little flamboyant coat. The one who thinks he will rule over us one day, the dreamer.

But after brief negotiations among his brothers, and some arm twisting by one, they agreed rather than killing Joseph to merely throw him in a pit where he could die a slow death. Be reminded, the pit they selected had no water in it. There was nothing there to sustain life even for a few days, let alone until he could possibly be recused (*cf.* Genesis 37:18). Perhaps damp, perhaps even dusty, but certainly damning, for without God's immediate intervention, death would be imminent, but such is the case in lives of the chosen. God not only has you thrown in a pit, he has you thrown in a pit with no sources of sustainability. Worse, often he personally throws you in the pit.

Having long range plans for Joseph however, God did intervene, but he intervened in a manner that was not exactly positive for Joseph, at least from a worldly perspective. He could have; he chose otherwise.

So his brothers draw Joseph from the pit, and Joseph is saved! Nope. Again, God chooses otherwise. They sell him to

Midianites for 20 shekels of silver.[20] Of course, the money was not what they wanted; ridding themselves of Joseph was, and this was the quickest way to do it. But before Joseph begins accepting his fate with the Midianites, God intervenes again. Would he choose to have Joseph freed? Nope. He would choose otherwise. Joseph is sold yet again, this time to Potiphar, an Egyptian officer under Pharaoh. (*cf.* Genesis 37 forward)

As time settled in, Joseph would succumb to his fate of being a Hebrew slave. With no other choice, he served his Egyptian master, and served him well. He did his best to put forth that Sunday morning face that says, "Ain't God good." But to the called, to the chosen, God always has more in store before a life-changing ordeal like this is over, much more, so just as Joseph began to accept slavery as a way of life, he is thrown into prison when false allegations are levied against him by Potiphar's wife after Joseph refused her sexual advances. Now Joseph would suffer further. Not that slavery was good, but almost certainly, it was better than prison. So to the dungeon Joseph would go.

---

[20] Twenty shekels weighs approximately 8 ounces. Assuming all 20 ounces were 100 percent silver, Joseph was sold for what would equate to $184.00, today. Of course, the irony is heavy here, given that the one purchased for less than two hundred dollars would rise to become the leader of Egypt.

Even then, God was not finished with Joseph. He could have been; he chose otherwise. The chief cupbearer, whom Joseph had helped survive prison, now forgets Joseph's acts of kindness when he is brought before Pharaoh. He forgets who helped him survive prison, altogether. He regains his position of prestige but negates to fulfill the single request his friend asked him to do upon leaving prison. "Remember me when with Pharaoh." (*cf.* Genesis 40:14) When the cupbearer's life is restored, he forgets who foretold of this wonderful event of restoration, who interpreted his dream, altogether. The person who gave the cupbearer hope during dismal circumstances, the person who gave the cupbearer reason to live. Forgotten. Completely forgotten. Just used and discarded. So two additional years in prison came Joseph's way; remember, all after following his father's will.

Repeatedly, Joseph found himself suffering from the evil acts of others. Repeatedly Joseph is subjected to harsh and deliberate treatment—again, all after following the will of his father, a point I cannot stress enough. His brothers could have chosen to do the right thing; they chose otherwise. The Midianite traders could have chosen to do the right thing; they chose otherwise. Potiphar could have chosen to do the right thing; he chose otherwise.

Potiphar's wife could have chosen to do the right thing; she chose otherwise. Potiphar, again, could have chosen to do the right thing; he chose otherwise. The cupbearer could have chosen to do the right thing; he chose otherwise. Day after day, the people who mistreated Joseph rose to another opportunity of coming clean with their evil acts of disobedience and lies, and chose otherwise.

While others schemed; Joseph suffered. They lied; Joseph suffered more. They profited; Joseph paid the price. They laughed; Joseph wept. They looked for the limelight; Joseph sought the solitude of suffering. They went to the comforts of their families; Joseph was abandoned. They were prideful; Joseph was shamed. They scoffed; Joseph cringed. They lived big dreams; Joseph's dreams were shattered. They went on with their lives of leisure; Joseph scraped out a life of misery. They were elevated; and Joseph was broken.

Joseph followed his father's will that day, and suffered immensely for it. The calamity, the destruction, the scheming ways of his brothers lasted but a few minutes and it was over. The fallout remained.

Oh, God did eventually make Joseph ruler of Egypt. As Joseph rose that day in prison, little did he know that today would be his day of restoration, a day that only God could ordain, and how grateful he was. God had rescued him. After all this time, someone had remembered him. After all the deceit, after all the lies, after all the evil acts against him, God had removed him from the dungeon of degradation to the palace of prominence, all in a matter of seconds.

But even then, the fallout remained. The fallout was going nowhere. It would remain with Joseph the rest of his life. No, he was no longer a slave, nor a prisoner, but the fallout would follow him forever. Envied, hated, abandoned, forgotten, shammed, humiliated. And restored.

How was Joseph now to handle the fallout? How was he to merge his new life with his old life? I guess most would say he was blessed, but Joseph's blessings, if you will, well, they came with strings attached. His prior life was still there. It was there in the open for all to see. Forget that he was innocent; that never mattered to anyone but Joseph, anyway. Could he explain away his past to his new friends? Remember, for years his friends were not what society deemed normal, and certainly, they were not what society considered upper crust. No, his friends were fellow slaves and prisoners. Lowlifes, castaways, outcasts, reprobates; the people society looked down upon, regardless of guilt or innocence. At best, his friends were other slaves, and at worst, they were murderers and thieves. The forgotten ones, despite that they too were children of God. Joseph and his band of misfits were nobodies; they did not matter. Even Joseph's own brothers referred to him as the brother that was "no more." (*cf.* Genesis 42:36)

So just how was Joseph to handle the anguish associated with the mistreatment dealt by his brothers, the traders, a lying seducer, or Potiphar? After all, he had been robbed of life, itself. In fact, the best years of his life had been taken from him. What could have been was stolen from him. How was he to handle being sold out by his own family, by his own flesh and blood? How was he to handle being a former slave? Falsely accused in a despicable way? Or being falsely imprisoned? Try living with that. The stigma of being a slave, sexual deviant, and prisoner would follow him the rest of his days regardless how high he may rise in society; because again, no one cared about the truth but Joseph.

Any one of these issues is enough to make the strongest Christian cower, yet Joseph endured all simultaneously. He would rise every day with evil hanging over his head. The false accusations. The lies. The egregious deeds. Where he went, fallout followed. On his best day, people he knew would avoid him. They would walk out of their way not to acknowledge him, or shake his hand. They would gossip. They would take jabs at him. They would make little remarks reserved for lunch after church on Sundays. They would secretly stare at him as he struggled to remain hidden in the shadows. They would whisper in secret, quietly pondering whether there were any truths to the vicious rumors. "Yes, I wondered that, too. There he is, over there by the bush, the quiet one. I always thought he was kind of different, anyway."

Would Joseph be accepted? No, he would he be shunned. He would be looked down upon for no valid reason. He was just guilty. Before that? You know, before he was thrown in prison; what was he? Oh, before that? He was just some slave.

Joseph would be lifted from prison, indeed, but no indication is given that his sentence was officially pardoned. His record was never expunged. He was never declared not guilty, and he surely was never declared *innocent*. He was never allowed to present the truth. No one cared about the truth—except Joseph. The truth was what people wanted to believe; it was subjective, derived from the ever-changing gossip of the day. And once the deceitful accusations were made, Joseph was guilty. In fact, Joseph would indeed be considered guilty the rest of his life, despite the truth.[21]

Not to belabor the point, but these points are crucial to understanding the voluminous issues with which Joseph dealt. His own brothers abandoned him. His father thought he was dead. Traders sold him. Potiphar's wife accused him, and the cupbearer did not remember him. Joseph was indeed "no more." Certainly, all of these people could not be wrong. "That Joseph, well you know, I am not saying he is a bad person, but I mean, based on everything, he surely looks like he'd be a problem. I mean, his own brothers hated him. The man was a worthless slave; then they threw him into prison for attempted rape; against Potiphar's wife, no less. And from what I hear, apparently even his fellow prisoners there would have little to do with him."

---

[21] And what would happen to those who schemed and lied against Joseph? Oh, them? Nothing; not a thing. They went on to ruin the lives of others. To the contrary, however, those who ruined Joseph's life through their schemes and lies should have had to suffer, each to the full extent they caused Joseph to suffer—in the same manner, and then some, until their punishment began.

Throughout his lifelong ordeal, Joseph's interpretation of blessing would become a derivative of the lens he used during interpretation. As a pit-dweller, as a slave, as the accused, and as a prisoner, was Joseph waiting on death, or was he walking toward greatness, toward significance? Joseph's success would become a derivative of how he navigated failure, so how he framed his walk would make every difference in his understanding of his struggles and subsequent suffering. The same holds true today. How we frame our walk, how we navigate failure, makes every difference regarding whether we gain deep understanding and wisdom as we move toward significance, or we live a lifetime of bitterness, the drink of poison we take when expecting it to eliminate those responsible.

No doubt as you have surmised from these readings, footnotes, and implicit and explicit attitudes and jabs thereof, I too have been greatly wronged by more than one person, or being, in life, so I too understand the struggles of couching cowardly events of darkness against me as anything positive. Indeed, it is no easy task, as regardless, the fallout remains; it lingers. It is there, regardless how I frame it, and it stares ready to destroy me dare I drink the poison.

No matter how Joseph hoped to the contrary, no matter how many times he prayed to the contrary, fallout remained. It haunted him. It made his days long, and his nights longer. Joseph was left only to decide how he would deal with the fallout. He could walk through fire and live a lifetime of bitterness. Or, he could walk through fire and gain understanding, deep understanding that leads to Godly wisdom and eventual significance. Either way, *he would walk through the fire*, and he would be burned. How badly he was burned depended entirely on his response.

Jesus expounded upon these type events in the parable of reaping and sowing, but what we most often overlook is that, if we indeed reap what we sow, at least to some extent and in somewhat of a twisted manner, we control the harvest (Gal 6:7). This does not mean that Joseph deserved his misgivings, not by any means. Life was full of twists and turns completely out of his control. However, his understanding became an output of the methodologies he employed for interpretation of blessing. In other words, Joseph's perception of blessing meant everything if he was to gain understanding that led to wisdom, and eventual significance.

Of course, the same applies to us. Have you too sat Sunday after Sunday listening to sermons with no substance? Or listening to the so-called wisdom of others with no depth? Much breadth; no depth. These messages ramble for miles and miles, only to scratch the surface of nothingness. There are only a couple of possible reasons for such shallowness. The messenger has never walked through an extended fire that resulted in deep spiritual understanding and subsequent Godly wisdom, and/or two, the messenger does not allow the Holy Spirit to speak through him, choosing rather to speak on his own behalf. Both are missed opportunities for the messenger and the listener. You can hear it every Sunday morning all across America. Oh, we hear breadth, lots and lots of breadth, just no depth. The breadth barely touches the surface.

Continuing our attempt to understand blessing through the trials of Joseph, however, from a secular perspective managing the distribution of Egypt's grain supply appears to be a noble, yet simple endeavor. However, an endeavor of this magnitude in Joseph's day was much different from the magnitude of such in our day. While the Egyptians were excellent engineers and constructors in their day, though much of their practice was learned through trial and error, modern day logisticians and managers were not so well versed as to be able to manage grain collection, storage, and distribution over the seven years of plenty and subsequent seven years of famine. Computer hardware and software were not available. Our modern-day transportation systems were not at their disposal, nor were modern day grain bins, elevators, or conveyors. They certainly were not equipped to deal with large systems engineering problems such as the food supply of a country, and more importantly, the Egyptians were not yet experienced in what today would be referred to as socialism, for until this point, remember, it was every family for themselves—capitalism. If you wanted to eat, you worked—quite contrary to what Egypt would soon become; and what America has become in recent decades. Like Egypt, the United States has become a socialist country where the takers far outnumber the makers. Neither were the Egyptians equipped to handle the corruption that would come with a government-controlled food supply. Then again, neither would be, or is, the United States.

Let me digress a minute to demonstrate how corruption plays out in governments around the world, including the United States, with a couple of basic examples. Around four years ago I conducted a preliminary feasibility study for the president of a Sub-Saharan country that will remain nameless for the implementation of a multi-billion-dollar rail system that would traverse multiple Sub-Saharan countries. In fact, the rail project would open doors to intercontinental travel across much of Africa, a medium greatly needed.

The preliminary analyses included economic and financial analyses coupled with the necessary technical (engineering) components to conduct the economic and financial portions of the study; and after a year, I completed the work. We then were asked to handle all pending economic, financial, and technical studies, as well as management of all planning, engineering, and construction of what would eventually result in a project well over $50 billion. But good news travels fast, as they say, and other firms quickly attempted to establish themselves into the mix. And they did just that. Funny how a $77 million kickback to the top government official there suddenly made an Italian firm more competitive than mine.

This was not the first such government corruption I have witnessed in my life, however. Not by far. Another project involved a similar scenario, coal reserves, and the energy sector. But when essentially what would be referred to as a dictator in a country mandated that he be paid *personally* through kickbacks for all coal reserves we used to energize several energy projects—energy that his own country would use—we had no choice but to remove ourselves from the equation, even if it was against his will.

Corruption plays out every day in the US, as well, just slightly less conspicuously. Sometimes it involves money and greed, and other times it does not. In any case, it always involves sin on the part of Godless leaders. Consider what we have witnessed in the US at the federal level in the last few years, and remember, these are only the things we know:

Demilitarization of the United States
Lack of Serious Border Control
Internal Revenue Cover-up
Keystone Pipeline Prohibition
GSA Uncontrolled Spending
Uncontrolled Lavish White House Spending
Premature Removal of Troops from the Middle East
Illegal Immigration
Beheadings & Mass Killings
Anti-Christian Activities & Stands
Jeremiah Wright Controversy
Anti-Israel Attitudes & Stands
One Million Dollar Obama Tour Bus
Pro-Islamic Activities
Iranian Nuclear Armament
AIG Scandal
Collapsed US Economy/Collapsed World Economy

Cash-for-Clunkers Program
Sequestration
Solyndra/ General Motors
High Unemployment
Unaccountable Police Corruption
Appointment of Czars
Wars & Terrorism
Attempted Gun Control
Eric Holder Corruption
Uncontrolled Government Spending & National Debt
Anti-American Employment Growth Policies
Increased reliance on Welfare/Move toward to Socialism
Anti-American Foreign Policies
Benghazi Cover-up
Obamacare Mandate/Attempted Hobby Lobby Mandate
Veterans' Affairs Cover-up
AP Phone Records Scandal
Removal of Historical US Facts

So, you see, a country's food supply had to be managed by a Godly man, much unlike what we see in our governmental and political structures today, and society at large. He must be God-centered and thus, selfless; again, much unlike what we see in government today. To manage a nation's food supply, he must be a man able to manage calamity, and chaos. He must understand pain, and suffering. He must understand what it is like to have everything. And to have nothing. And conversely, he must understand what it is like to have nothing, and have everything. He must understand the satisfaction that comes with going to bed with a full stomach and the acceptance of not going to bed at all. He must understand and be able to manage poverty, lowliness, and meekness and simultaneously, immense power, control, and prestige. He must understand the deep desires of bitterness and revenge, coupled with the necessities of self-control. He must have a finely tuned discerning spirit. He must have the courage to fulfill God's will under extreme circumstances, even when all endeavors act against him. He must have the resolve to fulfill God's will, even when he walks alone. He must understand popularity and fame, and isolation and loneliness. He must understand acceptance, and rejection. And he must understand certainty, and insecurity; what it means when God says no, and what it means when God says yes.

Had it not been for Joseph's discerning, obedient spirit, Egypt would have starved to death, and God's people would have perished, for "Where there is no vision, the people perish." (Proverbs 29:18) Had an unproven man, an untested man, a man who had not been through the fire over and over, been placed in charge of a nation's food supply, the Israelites and Egyptians would never have survived the seven years of plenty, let alone the seven years of famine. As they say, show me a thousand men who can handle adversity, and I will show you one man who can handle success.

Retrospectively, managing Egypt's grain supply was not the central concern, you see; leading and managing God's people was. And such could occur only through one who was divinely chosen, only through one who had been beaten into shape, not gently refined.

God did his greatest work in Joseph so he could later do his greatest work through Joseph. Jesus himself offered the best example of this. How else would we have eternal life had he not first endured the walk to Calvary, died, and been raised again? Through his death and resurrection, we have eternal life (*cf.* John 3:16). Through Joseph, God saved a nation. Through Noah, God saved the world, and through Jesus, God saved humanity.

Herbert M Barber, Jr, PhD, PhD

The Call Remains

The call remains. Despite all, the call remains. "For the gifts and the calling of God are irrevocable."[22] *Nothing more need be said. In reality, however, much more must be said.*

Perhaps no one understood these words more than Peter. God's call on Peter's life was irrevocable. The call had been rendered, and it was not reversible. Despite all, the call on Peter's life would remain. It would serve as a final immutable testament of the relationship between God and Peter.

Peter was in Jesus' inner circle and one of his closest confidants. He walked with Jesus. He traveled with Jesus. He ate with Jesus. He slept with Jesus. He knew Jesus and knew him well. And Jesus knew him.

---

[22] Romans 11:29

God's calling on Peter would take him through many enviable situations, and many that were not so enviable. He witnessed the transfiguration presented in Matthew. He was there when God called out, "This is my beloved Son, with whom I am well pleased..." (Matthew 17:5). He was there when Jesus healed the woman from prolonged bleeding. He was there when Jesus raised the little girl from the dead, and of course, he was there when Jesus commanded him to come to him, to walk on water, a situation that would prove symbolic to Peter's entire life.

Without him, Peter could do nothing. Without him, Peter did nothing. "And Peter got out of the boat, and walked on the water and came toward Jesus. But seeing the wind, he became frightened, and beginning to sink, he cried out, 'Lord, save me!'" (Matthew 14: 29-30) Yet, despite his apparent confidence and obvious boldness, Peter remained faithful to Jesus. Despite his slip to the flesh here and there, Peter remained faithful to Jesus— until, well, he eventually learned that perhaps he was no more committed than the rest of Jesus' followers.

But, "Not all of you are clean." (John 13:11) As Jesus foretold of his pending death and resurrection, he became quite troubled, saying to his disciples, "Truly, truly, I say to you, that one of you will betray me." (John 13:21) How could such be possible? How could one turn his back on Jesus? After all they had experienced together? After witnessing Jesus perform miracle after miracle together? Moreover, how could one of *the chosen* turn on any of the others, let alone Jesus? Their master; their teacher; their Christ. How could one singled out from all others betray him? How could one of the chosen prove so contemptuous, so disloyal, and so despicable? How could one of the chosen sell out to the enemy? A deceiver. A traitor. Darkness. All for a few coins.

Leading up to the sellout of Jesus, however, Jesus' prediction of Judas' betrayal would serve somewhat satirically as a warning to another disciple who would also betray Jesus—Peter himself, the one who arguably knew Jesus better than all other disciples. The one Jesus referred to as, *the Rock*.[23] (Matthew 16:18) The one who humbly but boldly confessed to Jesus, "You are the Christ, the Son of the living God." (Matthew 16:16) The one who, only seconds before Jesus confronted him, too, fearlessly claimed, "Lord... I will lay down my life for You." (John 13:37) Yes, that Peter, the one who wasn't standing in line when God was passing

---

[23] There exists some debate in the theological circles as to Jesus' exact meaning in Matthew 16:18; such debate is not relevant to our case here.

out meekness and humility. Pretty much like many of us, but that's okay, for as we are about to see, God is big enough to handle such crass boldness on Peter's part. And mine.... And yours.

Jesus' response to Peter's boldness was telling, and it pierced the darkness. It had a marked truth about it. Perhaps his response was spoken softly with love, but it was deafening, and it was definitive. "Will you lay down your life for Me? Truly, truly I say to you, a rooster will not crow until you deny Me three times." (John 13:38) And a hush fell across the room.

The reprimand of all reprimands was handed down. How humbling. How humiliating. Not Peter. *The Rock* would never entertain such thoughts. He lived life steadfast in his commitment to Christ. "He who is not with me is against me." (Matthew 12:30) Oh, they may deny you, Lord, but, "...I will not deny you." (Matthew 26:35) Not me. "Remember our conversation a few minutes ago, Jesus? 'You are the Christ, the Son of the living God.' (Matthew 16:16) I will never deny you, for I am Peter."

The worth of such unsubstantiated boldness was soon to be revealed to Peter in a way that only Jesus could. It would be the single most important learning experience in the life of Peter, and subsequently, it would be a life-altering turning point in his life. He would learn more about commitment in this single experience than during all other times with Christ combined, times ten. Prior to today, it was only knowledge. Soon, however, it would be tempered; knowledge would become wisdom, and wisdom would begin sneaking up on significance.

As Jesus was again scolding Peter, James, and John in the Garden of Gethsemane for sleeping after he had instructed them to keep watch, the betrayer arrived, making way for the beginning of the end. As Jesus is seized, their paradoxical commitment to Christ is revealed. "...the disciples left Him and fled." (Matthew 26:56) They did not go with Jesus. They were weak. They fled. They vanished. When the time of reckoning came, they cowered, and they scurried. And as they cowered and scurried, they pondered their hypocrisy, all confident before their pending trial, only to scatter like flies when their time came to stand up and be counted.

But contrast the actions of the disciples with recent actions[24] of college students and their professor in Oregon who were asked

---

[24] 2015

one by one whether they were Christians. If they said no, they were allowed to live. If they said yes, a bullet was put in their head. Those who had walked with Christ in the flesh, those who had witnessed his miracles? They fled. Yet one by one, nine Christians who had never saw him stood tall as they took a bullet for Christ from a deranged boy not much older than most of his victims. Such begs serious theological inquiry, far past my spiritual depth.

But almost certainly, questions immediately set in among the disciples, especially in the bold one, Peter; oh yea, I mean, *the Rock*. After all, the disciples were but human. Was this man really the Christ, the son of the living God? Was he who he said he was? Was he who I said he was, and if he was, why did he not stop this nonsense? Call down a legion of angels and stamp out the darkness! Can he not save himself? Then, the obvious question. *How can he save us?* Their questioning would only lead to profound confusion and doubt as they crouched together without the presence of their confidante, their protector.

Almost certainly the doubt and confusion, the ambiguity, would settle into the pit of Judas' gut more than in any other disciple. After all, he was the betrayer himself. But moreover, he was a follower of Jesus, despite what you think of him.

When Judas "saw that He had been condemned, he felt remorse and returned the thirty pieces of silver." (Matthew 27:3) Other translations state that Judas was filled with "regret" over his actions. He was overtaken with twisted emotions. He had denied Jesus, his friend, his spiritual mentor, and moreover, his redeemer; and if it is possible to go beyond that, what was he to do now?

By the way, it is indeed to go beyond that. Judas had no other choice, and his suicide is evidence of such. So, before we act as judge, jury, and executioner of Judas, put yourself in Judas' situation. We have all walked in similar shoes at some point in our lives, and if the truth were told we have walked in these shoes more often than we care to discuss. The time people were bashing Christianity and you did nothing. The time someone mocked Jesus while you remained silent. Or on a somewhat simpler note, the time you remained silent when your kids were forced to study evolution while negating creation—and the creator—altogether. Like it or not, we all deny Christ on occasion. We may not outright deny him as we say Judas did while somehow suggesting that Peter did not, and we may not reject his salvation—and be cast into hell for doing so, but we certainly do not always stand up for him.

So, would you have stood up, friend? Would you have taken that bullet for Jesus? When you stared at your executioner in the face with the smell of death already in the air, would you? Would you take that bullet? Would you? Would I? "...whoever denies me before men, I will also deny him before my Father... (Matthew 10:33) Perhaps some things are better left untested.

In the case of Judas, he was so overtaken with the emotions associated with the sin that now engulfed him, that he hanged himself. (*cf.* Mathew 2) Give Judas some credit; at least he had remorse. In our denials of Christ, we just let it go, day after day after day, until we find ourselves living in a country filled with a sinful people who have no remorse for their intentions of destroying Christianity who are ruled by a tyrannical government intent on supporting them—and then wonder why our country has collapsed economically, socially, politically, and spiritually. We have reaped what we have sown, and for those who have read another one of my books, remember; if we indeed reap what we sow, in a twisted way, we also control the harvest.

Perhaps a personal example is due, one that fortunately did not involve death. I recently conducted a highly rigorous study for a government involving the statistical and "practical" effect a multi-billion-dollar infrastructure project would have on the US economy, coupled with sophisticated analyses regarding the technical, financial, and economic feasibility of implementing such a project. Projects such as this are always contentious, with supporters on one side and opponents on the other side, neither of which are your friend.

These projects become even more contentious when they are proposed in a day when economic hardship, political turmoil, and moral decay in our government is all around us. From a political perspective, these projects are touted as a means of increasing economic output in economies, such as increasing GDP, incomes, jobs, tax generation, and similar variables, but from a serious econometric perspective, such is often not the case. Unlike politicians and government employees however, we do not have the luxury of recommending taxpayers spend billions of dollars without feasibility of the project first being substantiated technically, statistically, financially, and econometrically, as in many cases we have proven these well-intentioned endeavors to be merely superfluous spending to the tune of billions. Subsequently, and no matter what, we are stuck in the middle with friends on neither side of the equation—pun intended.

As I wrapped up the final few days of their study a far-left reporter called to inquire as to statements I made in another book regarding the economic collapse of the United States. Unknown to me at the time, his inquiry was laced with evil intent shadowed with darkness, but generally he wanted to know if I stood by statements I previously rendered in that book. Before I had the opportunity to officially defend my statements, as every statement was far removed from its context, my face and name was plastered across several large newspapers and television stations in the US and abroad—for several weeks. It was even the topic of talk radio. The mayor of this particular city issued an ill-advised statement regarding my comments. He slandered his own consultant, the consultant who could, if desired, take every effort to slant his findings *against* the project, the project he and President Obama regularly touted as an economic stimulus during their local back-slapping events to promote the project.

I appeared as a fool, personally—and professionally. In the end, I was destroyed because I spoke the truth; ultimately because I stated that the United States has collapsed because we have disobeyed God by personally negating our relationships with him, and in so doing, we have sold out to the government. Such can be definitively determined; just parallel the last fifty years of the United States with the years leading up to, and through, captivity of God's people in the book of Exodus. Only the non-discerner will not see the obvious parallels, and like God's people who were in captivity 430 years for selling out to the government, there is no rescue for the US outside direct intervention by God, himself.

Over the course of several months, I was referred to across a host of media streams as a racist, bigot, and hater, all because I dared to enter God, the Bible, and very basic analyses into the equation. Colleagues, family, and friends living in other cities called me just to tell me they saw me on television or read about me in the newspaper, magazine, or some blog. Nearly a year after this occurred, I still receive calls. My own parents even called me to tell me they saw reporters on several television stations slamming me for my spiritual beliefs. And strangely, I saw an article regarding my comments in Al Jazeera, a state-funded newspaper in the Islamic country of Qatar. In retrospect, given that a few of my comments surmised that President Obama, an obvious strong Muslim supporter or Muslim outright, has regularly supported Islamic activities as he tramples on the deaths of American Marines and soldiers who fought against such darkness, I should not find it surprising that Middle Eastern nations would publish such. I offended one of their own.

When I delivered the study in full to the client, I was told my firm was terminated, despite the fact that we were finished with the study, in full, the fact that we had fulfilled every mandate established in our contract and then some, and the fact that they were very satisfied with our analyses; and of course, the fact that they used my analyses and accommodating recommendations to vote in favor of spending billions of *your* tax dollars. And funny; to date I have seen no one attempt to contradict the advanced econometric techniques I used in that investigation to forecast return on investment. Imagine that. Bold comments without the intellectual savvy to back it up.

So, how many people on the taskforce to whom I answered stood up for me when I was destroyed because of my personal belief in God's everlasting word, you ask? Did the chair of that taskforce stand up against their viciousness? You know, the chair, the multi-billionaire who was leading the charge of the taskforce. The one who stated, "I truly enjoyed working with Dr. Barber. He made a very complex assignment understandable." Or what about another member of the taskforce; did he stand up for me? The member who said, "Dr. Barber applied mathematical models to... a highly contentious multi-billion-dollar public sector project. His work is highly complex and very important in our decision to implement what is a huge financial undertaking." Or what about this member of the task force; did he stand up against the evils that so engulfed the entire study? The one who said, "Dr. Barber took on a very complex topic that will have economic implications across the United States for decades... [Speaking] as a fellow PhD researcher, Dr. Barber knows how to address controversial topics with rigorous analyses, analyzing the positive and the negative, thus allowing us to ponder many tough questions we had not considered as a committee." Or, what about Christians in the public or the very influential churches in this particular city; did they stand against such slanderous and seemingly endless comments against not only me, but God and his word? No. Sadly not a single person or entity stood to be counted with me during those weeks; not one person, not even Christians. Sadly, I considered some on the task force as friends, especially the chair. But be reminded, light always eventually trumps darkness. As the chair of the taskforce, a man I considered my friend, stated the day their completed analyses and recommendations were hand delivered, "Dr. Barber, your remarks might be truthful, but they are not politically correct." My reply to him said it all. "No, they weren't, but then again, the *Truth* rarely is."

Similarly, when it comes to being counted, Christian or otherwise, many people are just cowards, so let us use caution when we slam Judas for his betrayal of Jesus. Though not directly defending Judas, his sin is juxtaposed against my salvation, and presumably, his own. How fortunate for me.

Likewise, let us refrain from overzealous finger-pointing when it comes to how the disciples handled the situation during and following the actual betrayal. As for Peter, and I suppose the rest of the disciples, his confusion was closing in on wisdom. Knowledge was transforming into understanding, and understanding was transforming into Godly wisdom, and well, wisdom was transforming into greatness, into significance, all before his very eyes. Amongst the turmoil, amongst the questioning, and amongst the confusion, what it meant to be called, to be chosen, to be set aside, was soon to take on a new meaning.

"I do not know what you are talking about." (Matthew 26:70) Denial One. "I do not know the man." (Matthew 26:72) Denial

Two. And as Peter resorted to his days as a scruffy fisherman, he cursed and swore forcefully, "I do not know the man!" (Matthew 26:74) "And immediately a cock crowed." (Matthew 26:74) Denial Three. Then Peter remembered the words Jesus had spoken, "Before a cock crows, you will deny me three times." (Matthew 26:75)

With that, Peter wept. He was an emotional wreck. He was spent. In reality, Peter had now denied Christ not three times, but four; once in the Garden when he fled and the three times Jesus predicted. He had denied the most important person in his life. He had denied his friend. He had denied his Christ, the only one who could save him from certain damnation. His unshakable commitment as *the Rock* had been shaken to its foundation. And there, he found that perhaps even his own foundation was questionable.

In what would amount to minutes, Peter would realize the weaknesses in his foundation, or at least that such weaknesses existed. It would be akin to an engineer placing loads of 5,000psf on soils with bearing capacities of only 1,000psf, or perhaps stresses on beams that exceeded not only their allowable stresses but their yields, meaning that the beams are so overloaded that they have passed what is referred to as an elastic state into the point of no return, their plastic state.

After following Christ some three years, it all came down to a few swift decisions for Peter. Very quickly, he would learn that his unshakable confidence in his commitment to Christ Jesus was grounded only in the weakness of self, rather than the bedrock of Christ. And now, what amounted to a blip in his life would haunt Peter the rest of his life. "You see that a man is justified by works, and not be faith alone," (James 2:24) meaning a man is *validated* by works, and not faith alone.

The fallout from the hypocrisy of his denial would forever be etched in his mind, ever to remind Peter of his epic failure, of his own denial of Christ. And the fallout would linger. It would wait with baited breath to pounce on Peter with each day's passing. It would hit him on his bad days, and it would hit him on his good days. Always there, just to remind him of who he was.

The fallout would remain. He had denied Christ. That would never change. It would be there every time friend and foe alike heckled him with crows of roosters. But so would his call. The call on Peter's life was going nowhere. It, too, would be there, encouraging Peter to move forward, to complete that which God started, and reminding him of his limitations without God. Godly wisdom had overtaken knowledge, and yes, Peter would prevail.

Like Peter, deeply committed Christians find similar scenarios playing out in life. God allowed such calamity in Peter's life for many reasons, one of which that was foundationally fundamental to his spiritual growth; he is God, and you are not. He is God, and Peter, *the Rock*, well, you are not. Repeatedly prior to and during the *Exodus*, for example, the explanation from God following destruction is, "so you will know that I am God."[25] "...apart from me, you can do nothing." (John 15:5) Nothing; and we find this explanation from God as it relates to calamity and its associated fallout over and over in the God's word. In fact, we find little explanation other than this as it relates to life's immense struggles, even for life's most arduous difficulties we endure.

God allowed, or caused, calamity in your life for the same reason he allowed it in Peter's life; to give you an opportunity to know God, so you may know the depths of his heart. *Come now. I*

---

[25] *cf.* Exodus 6:7, 7:5, 7:17, 8:10, 8:22, 9:16, 9:30, 10:2, 14:4, 14:17, 14:18, 16:6, 16:7, and 16:12.

am offering you an opportunity. No other reason. He alone is enough. He is your strength. He is your sustainer. He is your provider, and he is your provision. Read that again. He is not only your provider; *he is your provision*. You need nothing else. "My grace is sufficient…" (2 Corinthians 12:9) Nothing else matters.

Joseph was abandoned by his family, sold into slavery, falsely accused, wrongfully imprisoned, denied reconciliation, and deliberately destroyed. Moses killed a man, feared for his life, lost his livelihood, and lived life as a field-hand. Noah was ridiculed and became a societal outcast under immense pressure as the only God-fearing man on earth. Peter denied Jesus four times, and Judas failed Jesus altogether.

Then again, Joseph lost over a decade of his life, only to save God's people from permanently perishing. Moses hesitantly surrendered his life, only to lead God's people to the Promised Land. Noah played the part of fool under severe adversity, only later to be the fulfillment of God's promises; and Peter saw weaknesses in his own spiritual foundation crumble while witnessing the fulfillment of the greatest blessing God would ever offer; eternal life. And Judas; well, he ushered in eternal salvation.

Perhaps the words of the great gospel legend Andrae Crouch sums up the lives of these men best:

I've had many tears and sorrows
I've had questions for tomorrow
There've been times I didn't know right from wrong
But in every situation
God gave me blessed consolation
That my trials come to only make me strong

Been a lot of places
And I've seen a lot of faces
There were times I felt so all alone
In my lonely hours
Those precious lonely hours
Jesus let me know that I was his own

Oh, singing through it all
Through it all
I've learned to trust in Jesus
I've learned to trust in God[26]

Through it all, through the mountains and the valleys, their calls would remain. When all else blew with the winds of change, their calls never wavered. And despite all associated with you, your call remains. Denial, divorce, adultery, murder, drugs, sex, alcohol, theft, lying, cheating. No matter. If God has called you,

---

[26] Through it All, as arranged by Gordon Motes, 2012, Songs I grew up singing. New Haven Records. Original lyrics and melody by Andrae Crouch.

your call remains. Either your call remains; we have grossly misinterpreted Romans 11:29 in and out of context; or Romans 11:29 simply is not true. Your gifts, and your calling, are *irrevocable*. Let's state that differently for those who are refractory by nature. *Your call is irrevocable*. According to God's word, your gifts and your calling can *never* be revoked.

As a classic example, many, many Christians overlook Romans 11:29 altogether when it comes to calling a pastor, deacon, or other spiritual leader. And perhaps, so do you, but while people overlook Romans 11:29, they hold fast to the characteristics required of pastors, deacons, and similar spiritual leaders established in 1 Timothy 3. Of course, I should say, people hold fast to *some* of the characteristics established in 1 Timothy 3, primarily those that have not impacted their own lives, such as divorce, something that more and more pastors unfortunately face today. How can "the husband of one wife" (3:2) be regarded as anything other than the husband's *commitment* to his wife? Otherwise there is limited value in Romans 11:29 for those who are divorced, but called; and it negates 2 Timothy 2:21, altogether.

Therefore, if a man cleanses himself from these things [dishonorable activities, as noted in 2:20], he will be a vessel for honor, sanctified, useful to the master, prepared for <u>every</u> good work. (commentary and emphasis mine)

God's call on that person's life was not negated with his divorce, not according to Romans 11:29. Further, if repentance has occurred, that man is a vessel of honor; he is sanctified, free from sin; declared holy—and useful to the master in *every* good work. Similarly, if we hold fast that divorced men cannot serve in positions of spiritual leadership, specifically as pastors, how do we explain away the thousands of pastors who love money or have children who go astray? Remember, these same passages also mandate that a pastor be free from the love of money (3:2), and that he manages his household well, including having children that are not only under control but who have dignity (3:4-5).

Further, what about the characteristic, or gift, of teaching (Titus 1:9; 2 Timothy 2:24) required by persons in these positions? As one who has spent decades in a formal classroom as a student, one who has taught at the doctoral level on very complex subject matter, and one who regularly has to teach clients the fundamentals of decision science as it relates to engineering, economics, and research so they have at least a remote chance of understanding our findings and recommendations, most pastors are horrible teachers; they simply cannot teach. In fact, most pastors have no education, at all, and many, many of those who claim to have an earned education merely have mail-order diplomas not worth the cost of the printing. Truly, it is amazing at the sheer volume of pastors who lie about their educations—or the lack thereof; and education is one thing you cannot disguise in front of the truly educated. It becomes obvious within seconds of them opening their mouths. Nanoseconds. Nonetheless, these men attempt to give the appearance of being *learned* while having never learned. How can they educate if they themselves have never been educated? How do they expect to preach if they cannot teach?[27] Yet they preach, and people apparently listen. How sad. Do you not find it as ironic that the requirements for those in spiritual leadership roles found in 1 Timothy 3 and 5 has a discussion regarding apostasy that results from deceitful spirits and doctrines (4:1) sandwiched between it in chapter 4? Read

---

[27] It is not enough to have the spiritual gift of teaching or preaching. To be effective, a call to teach or preach is also a call to prepare to teach or preach, coupled with the benefits derived from the Holy Spirit. Otherwise, the potential to fully utilize that gift is minimized and often worse, greatly diminished.

those passages. This is not coincidental; there are no coincidences with God.

Despite the issues with which we deal, and regardless as to what they are, for those God has called, the call remains.

Accepting the Call

"The word of the Lord came to Jonah the son of Amittai saying, 'Arise, go to Nineveh the great city, and cry against it, for their wickedness has come up before Me.'" (Jonah 1:1-2) Jonah left for Tarshish, instead.

Such is the case with many of us in life. Hearing the call is rarely the problem; accepting the call is. Even then, actually heeding his call and moving forward still awaits those called. Unfortunately, the stronger the spiritual gifts, talents, educations, and intellects of those called, the stronger the propensity to resist the call. Perhaps, such persons are so incredibly talented that they can do anything, or at least they believe this to be true, that anything sounds better than following God's request—especially when, as it always does, involves his people—and moreover, when it means that this person with such promise will be brought down, not revered and lionized. Thus, there is much resistance, making acceptance of the call a near impossibility.

Jonah had similar issues. The word of the Lord came to Jonah, telling him to go to Nineveh to warn its people of the sinfulness of their wicked ways. And, without hesitation Jonah fled to Tarshish. Not, I prefer not to go, God; not, let's discuss this; but "I'm not going." In fact, he did not even take time to tell God no.

Presuming Jonah was near Joppa at the time God called, he traveled in a completely different direction than God commanded. Rather than go to Nineveh as he was called, a mere three-day journey, he boarded a boat to Tarshish, miles away. As opposed to walking through the relative safety over land, with the operative phrase being "relative safety," he chose to risk his life on the perilous Mediterranean Sea, all the way to the southern tip of Spain.

You see, where Jonah was going really did not matter. The destination was of no relevance. He was fleeing the "presence of the Lord." (Jonah 1:3) Anywhere would suffice; anywhere but where God called him. Of course, lest we be too hard on Jonah, it is with merit that we consider exactly where God called him to go, something always over looked when the topic of Jonah is broached.

To Assyria. To modern day Syria. God directed Jonah to go directly to those who are beheading Christians in the Middle East today. That is where God called Jonah. And like today, they were a different breed, an evil people, prospering from that which was not theirs to prosper. Nineveh, that "...bloody city, completely full of lies and pillage. Her prey never departs." (Nahum 3:1) These people did not deserve forgiveness and grace.[28] Thus, they did not deserve Jonah, nor his prophetic teachings, so Jonah took measures into his own hands. He boarded a boat in Joppa and headed for Tarshish. Let these people rot in hell where they belong. Of course, to those whom God has called, such ill-advised endeavors are rarely without subsequent pain and suffering and never without consequences. Either way, you run the risk of ruin, either by those he called you to serve, or God himself.

As previously noted, to many, the stronger the called, the stronger the gifts and talents, the stronger the resistance. And the stronger the consequences, the worse the pain and suffering. In

---

[28] Refer to the *Book of Nahum* for insight into the city of Nineveh.

fact, modern day definitions of pain and suffering do not give pain and suffering its proper due. Pain for those called can be immense and the suffering can be extensive, and both can be long-lasting, and Jonah wanted no part of it.

In defense of Jonah, however, the text does not provide the details of Jonah's life before or after this time in his life to the full extent. God's word rarely does. Most often we are left to ponder, to draw inferences, to draw our own conclusions through discernment from the Holy Spirit and historical reference. But the hand of God was indeed upon Jonah, right? Certainly, but what we see God work for his good we do not always see as *our* good.

In any event, Satan need not waste his valuable time placing his attention on those running from God. The called can handle this area just fine. However, why Jonah fled is perplexing, of sorts. The people of Nineveh were a bad people, an evil city governed by an evil people who acquired its riches through the ill-gotten gain of others.[29] But was that enough for Jonah to not only discount God's calling but to negate it altogether?

---

[29]Despite gaining its wealth by stealing from others, and evil actions abounding, the government of Nineveh ironically thought it necessary to build a great wall around the city to protect itself against outsiders. Let the reader not confuse the

To me, it would have been. Do not worry, friend; I am speaking on your behalf, as well. Forget that the Assyrians did not deserve Jonah's good presence, nor God's message and forgiveness, Jonah ran a high risk of leaving Nineveh in a pine box. Yes, even with God on his side. Read that again, because you will never hear such raw truth on Sunday morning. Even with God on his side, Jonah ran the risk of death, his own. And if he didn't go, well, as he was about to see, he still ran the risk of death.

On our best day, we are human and thus, sinful. Like us, sin was all around Jonah, even in the Joppa area, where we presume he was when God called him to Nineveh. Had Jonah experienced run-ins with the Ninevites (Assyrians) in the past? Likely. Perhaps he had even experienced run-ins with God in the past over similar issues. Or, perhaps Jonah had heeded God's call in years' past and had tired of the difficulties associated with them. Perhaps following God had brought nothing but hardship, nothing but grief and struggle. Perhaps Jonah was talented. Perhaps he was gifted,

---

actions of the governmental leaders in Nineveh with the government leaders in America, though the similarities are eerily similar when noting that our own government cowers behind its own walls—badges, guns, glass walls, solid walls, counters, locked doors, immunity, and laws that were meant to protect government employees while controlling *We the People*. Be comforted though; "The Lord... will by no means leave the guilty unpunished." (Nahum 1:3) Amen.

very gifted. Perhaps he could lead a horse to water *and* make him drink. Perhaps Jonah felt he knew the Assyrians better than God. After all, God was in heaven; Jonah maneuvered in and around these dark shadows regularly in his attempts to avoid them. He knew their wicked ways. He knew of the shadows of their presence. Or perhaps Jonah did not need God; or viewed through our day, perhaps he only needed God on Sunday mornings, leaving the balance of the week to the execution of his own gifts and talents—and own outcomes.

We find additional credence regarding Jonah's decision to flee to Tarshish instead of heeding God's call to Nineveh when the ship he had boarded became unstable in the seas of the Mediterranean. (Jonah 1:4, forward) As Jonah's newfound shipmates sought him to call upon his god to calm the storm, the captain found Jonah not fearing for his life, not trembling, not cowering down, or even praying, but asleep, sound asleep. The storm was violent, the waves were high, the boat pitched, and the boat rolled. Jonah slept. Was he that tired? Was his faith in his god so strong that he feared not? Countless explanations can be hypothesized as to his response to this violent storm, a storm that God himself orchestrated.

After the captain beckoned him on deck and lots were drawn, Jonah did not call upon God to calm the seas; his shipmates did. Jonah was stoic. In fact, he appeared apathetic, altogether. No opinion whatsoever. He was content being thrown overboard, left to the perils of the sea. Jonah no longer feared God, and likewise, he no longer did not fear God. Apathy appears to have taken over his love for God and his distaste for God, a reality witnessed by many who become lost in the trials of life. Jonah had lost his zeal of seeing God's people repent, or at least people he deemed unworthy, especially those who hated Israel. At the moment, he no longer cared either way, for God or his will. Even later, after Jonah cries out to God from the belly of the fish, and goes to Nineveh, Jonah seems content with God taking his life. (Jonah 2, forward)

So apathy lingered. It filled the belly of the whale. And it hung heavy in the air as he was spat upon the beach—and thereafter.

Despite being removed from certain death inside the belly of a whale, Jonah's fulfillment of God's call seemed to be laced with apprehension and misgivings on the part of Jonah. Read the text closely. Realistically paraphrased, "I may fulfill your call God, but I do so reluctantly against my personal desires and better judgment." Such disdain and reluctance for this particular call shows itself in Jonah after he finally yields to God's will, preaches, and the city of Nineveh repents, as well. Through it all, however, Jonah would realize that fleeing from God only brings one full circle—back to God.

Accepting God's call is never an easy endeavor to the chosen, or gifted, but as daunting as the possibility of being destroyed by an evil people is, or being eaten alive by a sea creation of the deep,[30] nothing compares to the call God placed on the life of Abraham. Nothing; yet Abraham's response could have not been more different. So, not to be redundant, but look at Abraham again briefly, this time from a slightly different perspective, that of accepting God's call.

Foremost, we find God himself intent on testing Abraham, not Satan, in Genesis 22, a fact worth remembering. Initially, God calls out to Abraham, "Abraham!" Abraham responds by saying,

---

[30] Debate abounds among scholars, theologians, and practitioners as to whether the story of Jonah being swallowed by a large fish in fact occurred, or being swallowed by a large fish metaphorically represents the difficulty associated with his call. Of course, it is indeed telling that we trust God to save our souls from eternal damnation, but by no means could we believe he could save a man from a fish—that he created! Let the reader not be misled; this debate is irrelevant to the central thesis presented within the story of Jonah.

"Here I am," as if God did not know where he was.[31] Following this, though, the situation turns ugly. It turns into a scene found only in the horror stories of wicked people. With no small talk, God instructs Abraham to take his son Isaac to the land of Moriah and offer him as a burnt offering. How could a good god mandate such an absurd request? Take the son you gave me and kill him? The son you gave me at one hundred years of age? How could this be? The god I have faithfully served all these years. God Almighty. No, the text notes no exchange such as this. There is no discussion as there was with Moses; there is no debate. Neither was there fleeing as there was with Jonah. Abraham did not immediately pack his bags and head in the opposite direction. Nor did he go fussing all the way. No, he rose early in the morning knowing he was going, split a few pieces of wood, saddled his donkey, and left with his son and two servants to a mountain yet to be determined. God neglected to tell him the specifics, the trivial things that stretch your faith even farther. Just take the son you longed for to the land of Moriah and offer him as a burnt offering; I will fill you in on the details later (*cf.* Genesis 22:2).

---

[31] Interestingly, this same exchange occurs between God and Moses in Exodus 3; and others. However, though nearly identical, the response from Moses and Abraham is likely more accurately viewed as a demonstration of their subservient role to God, rather than noting their geographical locations.

So, "On the third day Abraham raised his eyes and saw the place from a distance." (Genesis 22:4) Now having seen more detail of God's plan unfold, at least the specific location where he would slaughter his son, Abraham and Isaac scaled the mountain, dragging along wood for the alter. Then one of the most bittersweet exchanges in the Bible occurs. Realizing there was no sacrificial lamb, Isaac, through the faith that only a child can render, says to Abraham, "My father!" Daddy. To which his daddy responds, "Here I am my son," as if to compassionately console his son in his arms as only a loving daddy can. "I know. I understand, son. I too am saddened, very saddened. I too am distraught. I hurt for you. I hurt with you. And I would rather hurt in your place."

This is his son, his flesh and blood. What a grievous situation this must have been. He was only human. Certainly, Abraham was distraught. He was beside himself. Likely, he could barely walk, let alone scale a mountain under such extreme mental and physical anguish. And now, after desperately wresting his own demons to deny the call, his young son begins to realize that there is a very serious problem, one that will be resolved only through him. As if it were even possible, the darkness around the daddy and his son grows darker; grief worsens. Desperation delves to a new depth, a depth never experienced by Abraham, let alone his young son Isaac.

"Behold, the fire and the wood, but where is the lamb for the burnt offering?" Feel these words. Allow them to permeate the depths of your very soul. This was *his* son, and he was *his* father, *his* daddy. His life-giver, his protector. As God called down from Heaven after Jesus was baptized, "This is *my* son, in whom I am well pleased." (Matthew 3:17) No, words do no justice to the anguish here. Somehow however, despite the unspeakable turmoil engulfing the question, Abraham seems to respond with authority. "God will provide for himself the lamb for the burnt offering, my son." (Genesis 22:8) "Let us continue to walk."

How could Abraham muster the strength to remain strong in the mist of certain death? Not even his death, but that of his own son. And he would be the one taking it. There exists only a single way, for there was no other way. Abraham's spirit was so in tune with God's spirit that his will aligned perfectly with the will of God, even given the circumstances. What God orchestrated, who was Abraham to undo it? Who was he to test the will of God, let alone contradict it? God's will, and every result thereof, had become the will of Abraham, just as Jesus' denial of his will in the garden painfully surmised, "Not my will, Father, but thine be done."

Like most of us, Jonah put his will over His will, but not Abraham. Abraham put the will of his father over that of his will, and in so doing, obedience trumped understanding.

Living the Call

Arguably, nothing is more difficult than living a call that God places on one's life, especially for those whom he calls to fulfill challenging tasks.

*F*or those who live the Christian walk superficially, perhaps reading their Bible once in a while, praying as a need arises, attending church, and going about their day, they never truly know the depths of their maker; they never really know God, let alone understand him. Unfortunately, or perhaps fortunately, with the exception of very few, this description is reflective of most Christians. Their most difficult day involves issues that occur to every person, Christian or otherwise; finding money to pay past due bills, putting food on the table, juggling family and career, dealing with a disgruntled colleague, supervisor, or spouse, managing a health issue, dealing with a wayward child, or caring for an elderly friend or family member.

Conversely, however, those whom God has chosen to fulfill very specific callings will be pushed to extremes they never knew existed, let alone willingly sought; and they will appear as fools more often than not. No, we are not referring to the Sunday morning preacher who a day or two before crams together some ill-prepared shallow message he professes to be anointed by God. Nor are we referring to those preachers who, Sunday after Sunday, feel it is their responsibility to make their claim to fame through jokes or their ability to prosperity-preach; or to fill their fifteen minutes of fame with thunderous sermons sounding the goodness of God, or his never-ending love, support, and compassion. No, in fact, we are not referring to most modern-day preachers, at all. We are referring to persons whom God has chosen, those who he has set aside for very specific purposes, and sometimes, for very specific purposes never fully known. These people, God's chosen, will live their call filled with difficulty greater than you will ever hear on Sunday mornings.

The sad irony here is that there should be fewer of the former and more of the latter. Unfortunately, we no longer witness fire and brimstone messages in sermons or print that present God as he is; we would rather discuss Jesus' goodness, and more pointedly, what he has "done for me lately." In fact, there is nothing thunderous about most sermons these days, unless they are self-serving. No one speaks of who God really is; no one discusses the fact that he regularly struck down people with whom he felt the need. No one speaks of the God who had hundreds or thousands of babies slain, the God who offered his blameless servant over to Satan himself, or the God who allowed his own angels to procreate with humans. No one speaks of the God who allowed your family member to pass at the hands of some ill-advised decision some stranger made, or the evils thrown upon you every day by an evil psychopath, despite your pleas to God for the contrary. No, we prefer to discuss the Jesus of Nazareth, not the God of Abraham. Subsequently, we negate much of the central thesis of God—who he is, and what he expects from us.

Oh, we love the story regarding how Jesus filled the disciples' nets with fish when we needed the income. We love to hear how God parted the Red Sea and our enemies were engulfed. And we love to hear how a compassionate Jesus turned water into wine or fed five thousand people from essentially nothing when nothing was all we had. But what about the god who refused to allow the man who led God's people to the Promised Land to actually enter the Promised Land himself? You remember; the man God allowed to fulfill his life's ambition of herding sheep for decades in the middle of nowhere with no goals nor objectives in life other than waiting to die; the man who risked his life to deliver people from more than four centuries of bondage; the man who suffered every day of his miserable existence for decades in a wilderness that was geographically close to the Promised Land, all because God chose him. You know this man, the man who despite decades of supreme sacrifices, God refused to allow him entrance into the Promised Land—all because he struck a rock? Seriously? Over a single sin? Do we hear of this god?

What about the man God allowed to be sold into slavery, falsely accused of sexual misconduct, and falsely imprisoned; with no consequences to the liars and evil doers? Are there no consequences to those engulfed in raw evil? Do we hear of this god? What about the god who allowed the police in New York City recently to kill a man by suffocating him, and then be hailed as some form of pseudo-hero because he stopped a man from selling individual cigarettes on the street? Or the god who allowed a judge to destroy a family with no repercussions to the corrupt judge? You know, the judge who not only destroyed your family but simultaneously teaches Sunday school every Sunday morning at your church, the one who is lauded by your pastor and fellow worshipers because, after all, he is "the judge," a public servant, just facilitating justice against his version of evil doers, despite facts only to the contrary. This god; do we hear of him on Sunday mornings? Do we discuss this god? No, of course not; but we certainly hasten to paradoxically explain away his actions.

This, friend; this is the god with whom the chosen must deal in their resolve to live their call. This man travels the road less traveled, the one only few know. He walks in the freezing rain, and he walks in the sweltering heat, and he does so alone. His road is not paved, and he has no map. In many seasons, there is even no path. No one has been there prior to his travels to stomp down the thorny brush or flush out the vicious predators. He cuts the path as God directs, if and when he directs, and in the interim the weariness of the path that seeks to destroy him, only hardens him, ever so eventually; very, very slowly drawing him to God in ways only the downtrodden and destroyed have opportunity to experience.

As a man was sleeping one night in his cabin, suddenly his room filled with a great light, and God appeared. The Lord told the man he had work for him to do, and showed him a large rock in front of his cabin. The Lord explained to the man that he was to push against the rock with all his might.

So this, the man did, day after day. For years he toiled from sun up to sundown, his shoulders set squarely against the cold, massive surface of the unmoving rock, pushing with all his might.

Each night the man returned to his cabin worn and tired, feeling that his whole day had been spent in vain. As discouragement settled in, Satan decided to enter the picture by placing thoughts into the man's weary mind. "You know; you have pushed against that rock for a long time, and it has not moved a bit." With that, the man became very depressed; he even thought he was a failure. "Why, this task is downright impossible," said Satan. Now completely dejected, these thoughts discouraged and disheartened the man altogether.

Satan said to the man, "Listen, why kill yourself over this? Just put in your time, give a little effort, and that will be good enough." Sounding like a good idea, the weary man planned to do just that, but before doing so, he decided to take his troubled thoughts to the Lord.

"Lord," he rationalized, "I have labored long and hard in your service, putting all my strength to do that which you have asked of me. Yet, after all this time, I have not even budged that rock. What is wrong? Why have I failed?"

The Lord responded compassionately, "My son, when I asked you to serve me and you accepted, I told you that your task was to push against the rock with all of your strength, which you have done."

"Never once did I mention to you that I expected you to actually move the rock. Your task was simply to push the rock. And now you come to me with your strength spent, thinking you have failed."

"But, is that really so? Look at yourself. Your arms are strong and muscled, your back shiny and brown; your hands are callused from constant pressure, and your legs have become massive and hard."

"Through opposition, you have grown much, and your abilities now surpass that which you had. True, you haven't moved the rock. But your calling was to be obedient and push the rock, fully trusting in me. That you have done. Now, my son, I will move the rock."[32]

Chosen, called, or just living the dream, of the thousands of prayer requests you have rendered over the years, of all these countless pleas, how many has God responded in a manner you would deem affirmative? Be honest with yourself. Very few. Rarely do we receive what we ask. Rarely do we receive what we plea, regardless of the dire circumstances. No, not most of the time, not some of the time; rarely. How long we pray and how fervently we pray most often matters not in terms of God granting our request. No matter how much we believe nor how much faith we possess. Oh, God still works miracles, every day. He still answers prayers. Consider how God reminded me of this very thing only a few short months ago.

I have always spent time in prayer and Scripture in the mornings, and for some time, I have wrestled with this very

---

[32] Author unknown; reworked by H. Barber.

concept, that no matter how faithfully I prayed, God seemed to answer little. Then at night, well, I am ready for bed, so I pray little. However, as I do every night, one night recently I asked God to take care of my children and family, at large, during the night. I always ask God to protect them physically, mentally, psychologically, and spiritually, and that night was no different. But little did I know that in a few short hours God's faithfulness to me would come full circle in a way only he could orchestrate.

The phone rang around 5:30 that Sunday morning when my son got through to us. Of course, before we answered we knew something was wrong. He had fallen asleep on his way to work around five, driven off the right side of the rode into the ditch, barely missed a culvert, swerved back across the road, jumped a five-foot embankment on the left side of the road, and flipped his truck a few times. So, as I drove to the accident that morning, some 45 minutes away, I thanked God over and over that Brandon was okay, that it was not worse.

As I rounded the corner of a county road, just as the sun was penetrating the darkness, off in the distance I could make out the figure of my son standing beside a truck lying on its top, wheels toward the sky, beaten to pieces, as it rested in a peanut field. And just as I caught a glimpse of Brandon and his truck, it was as if God rolled me over, as well. I hear his words as clearly today as I did that morning. "So, do you still think I don't answer your prayers?"

What a powerful reminder that morning was for me. Somehow, through all the unanswered prayers, God was still in control. He was still there, and he was still faithful.

But do not misunderstand the reality of my argument; take it for what it is worth. Unfortunately, the probability that God will not respond to your prayer in what you consider affirmative is statistically significant at *any* alpha level. In other words, the chances that he will answer your request is nearly negligible altogether. Ever heard that on Sunday mornings during your weekly dose of feel-good? On occasion, yes, he does respond in what we consider the affirmative, and we are oh so grateful for these answers. But more often than not he does not respond at all. I know not why; he just does not. Why are most people going to spend eternity in hell? More perplexing, if heaven were perfect, why would God create humans knowing nearly all would ultimately reject him, opting rather to spend forever in the pits of hell?

This is a complex construct, one that baffles even the strongest of Christians. Why, as I pen these very words, did I receive word that my longtime friend from high school, Anne, would finally surrender to three bouts of cancer at barely 50? Why would such a sweet Godly woman be called home, only to leave behind two children whom she labored to bring into this world?

She and her family did everything right. She grew up in a Godly home with a Godly family, she accepted Christ at an early age, she did not partake of harmful drugs, drink, or smoke, she was active in her church, she was a Godly wife, and she reared Godly children. I know Anne; she gave more than she ever received. In everything she did, she exemplified God. She was a model servant of Christ. Yet life was snatched from her, and us, after fifty short years. How could this be anything other than wrong?

A few years ago a childhood friend struggled through yet another round of cancer treatment at Emory in Atlanta. Why? He was only in his 40s. He had every reason to live. A God-fearing family, wife, and two teenage daughters. Yet as Monty wrestled with his own pending death and eventual eternity, without warning his father Dub was diagnosed with Stage IV lung cancer, only to pass away a few days before Monty. A shattered family of women was left with no father, no husband, no brother, and no son. Why?

Man has pondered such injustices since the beginning of time. Surely Adam and Eve questioned this very issue when Cain killed Abel. The writer of Ecclesiastes also questioned such injustices. I question similar injustices, especially those without recompense or where there is no value in the loss; and like me, the writer found nothing but more injustice and darkness in places where justice was supposed to be levied. "...I have seen under the sun that in the place of justice there is wickedness, and in the place of righteousness there is wickedness." (Ecclesiastes 3:16) That, friend, is a very powerful observation.

However, I no longer feel obligated to explain events like this away. I no longer attempt to explain away the actions of God. I am not in that position. That is God's position. God only rarely responds the way I request. Horrible things happen to great people every day. People die only to spend eternity in the flames of hell, forever and ever and ever. Marriages and families are destroyed. People are destroyed through no fault of their own. Horrible things happen. Very horrible things happen, especially to the chosen, but as God clearly spoke to me one morning while yet again quizzing him on such difficult subjects, "Only when you stop trying to understand me and simply start obeying me, will you understand me." Wow. Just wow.

As Father Cavanaugh exclaimed in the movie, *Rudy*, as young Rudy Ruettiger earnestly prayed for acceptance into the University of Notre Dame to play football for the Irish, "Son, in 35 years of religious study, I have only come up with two hard incontrovertible facts: there is a God, and I'm not Him." How uncommonly profound; and in a movie, no less. He is God, and I am not; let it be. My understanding must always be trumped by my obedience, coupled with his grace, though paradoxically, my understanding can only be found through both.

Thus, if you are chosen, if you seek him with all of your being, your walk with God will be difficult. At times, it will be arduous, and very often it will be without understanding. In many cases, your walk will be alone; and it will be lonely. The rock upon which you push may never move, yet you will push obediently. Contrary to what you hear on Sunday morning in your feel-good service, you accepted Christ as your personal Savior to be spared eternal damnation in the pits of hell, not so God would make your life pleasant. Be reminded of that. And you accepted his call in obedience, and now you must fulfill that call in obedience. Not because you like the idea, or even want to, but because you are obedient.

> For the dream comes through much effort... When you make a vow to God, do not be late in paying it, for he takes no delight in fools. *Pay what you vow.* (Ecclesiastes 5:3-4, emphasis mine)

The unfortunate reality is that we most often have been presented only partial scriptural truths over the years, which of course, makes for a complete lie. We have become so acclimated to expecting only what we consider as God's goodness that we consider it a right, an entitlement. Such has become so prevalent in recent years that apostasy of the committed believer has become relatively easy, and to some extent, even easier for the strongest believer, especially when we are thrown a few serious curves on top of life. Then again, why would there not be a falling away from the church and sound biblical teaching? We offer everything yet we offer so little.

Our churches offer elaborate facilities, with many having not only main worship centers and ample classroom space, but also multiple campuses with worship centers, sanctuaries, chapels, fellowship buildings with large commercial kitchens, full-court gymnasiums that convert to support volleyball and other activities, daycare, schools, and colleges, counseling centers, recovery centers, retirement communities, and senior care centers. We have church bookstores, libraries, and studies. We have activities for babies, bouncers, crawlers, walkers, talkers, young people, college people, single people, married people, old people, divorced people, people who wish they were married, and even people who wish they were not married. We offer food for the homeless and food for the saints. We offer mothers' morning out, date night, book night, and game night. We offer everything a person remotely interested in church could want except the one thing they need most. *The Truth*. The one thing people seek, we deny them. Yet, as corrupt as society has become, most people still hold fast to the idea that something greater than humankind is in control. What irony.

Today we offer people all the subsidies with no substance. So to complement, not augment, our elaborate facilities and never ending offerings and caterings for all who ever thought about being, preachers, teachers, and counselors finely sift the Scriptures searching for something portraying Jesus' gentleness coupled with his infinite plethora of goodness to present them. After all, how could they not? We have granted the believer and unbeliever everything else; all creature comforts and then some. How uncomfortable we may become to know God for who he really is. The God of Abraham? The God of Joseph, Jonah, or Job? Forget it. We have boldly presented God's goodness for so long while negating to present him for who he is that we have forgotten that our comfort is not foremost on his mind. Neither is our fortune and fame. Consider God's charge to Ezekiel.

Son of man, I am sending you to the sons of Israel, to a rebellious people who have rebelled against me; they and their fathers have transgressed against me to this very day. I am sending you to them who are stubborn and obstinate children, and you shall say to them, "Thus says the Lord God." As for them, whether they listen or not—for they are a rebellious house—they will know that a prophet has been among them. And you, son of man, neither fear them nor fear their words, though thistles and thorns are with you and you sit on scorpions; neither fear their words nor be dismayed at their presence, for they are a rebellious house. But you shall speak my words to them *whether they listen or not*, for they are rebellious. (Ezekiel 2:3-7, emphasis mine)

Certainly, Ezekiel's comfort was not foremost on God's mind when he levied this charge. Neither was his fortune and fame. Ezekiel was charged with speaking directly to a people who had replaced God in their lives for the pleasures of disobedience, very closely to what has happened in the US over the last 50 or 60 years.

Consider what God said about his own people. Paraphrased with my personal emphasis, "They are a rebellious, stubborn, and obstinate group, and remember, they rebel against me to this day, so expect them to toss everything they have at you. Expect them to have no respect for you. After all, if they have no respect for me, why would you think they would respect you? But whether they listen to you is irrelevant; you are to speak to them. So, stand up son; it's time to be counted. And I'm doing the counting."

For those chosen, those who God sets aside, your life likely will be a perpetual struggle similar to that noted here with Ezekiel.

These will be the people you face daily. It will not be as we hear on Sunday mornings during our feel-good fix of creature comfort where soothing verses of Jesus' goodness are sprinkled with humor. There will be seemingly senseless ills brought upon you by yourself, others, Satan, and even God. Did you hear me? Even God; and if you still do not believe me, ask Job, or just sit with me one day. Or ask a host of others noted in God's word. Of course, some things will be rosy, all nice and peachy on occasion, but many, many areas of our lives will remain troublesome. Even your basic objective in life will often appear unclear. At other times, it may appear unclear altogether. Again, however, it is what it is. Let it be. *We need not understand to obey.*

For example, we do not know why God chose Moses, yet of all the persons living at the time, he did. He could have chosen others, anyone other than him, yet he chose Moses, a murderer. And he chose him at an appointed time in Moses' life. Not before, not after, but at a very specific time, some 40 years after he killed the Egyptian. Perhaps Moses had finally accepted his fate of herding animals. Then God came knocking. He had other plans, a plan which Moses had unknowingly been preparing to orchestrate for 80 years. In that choosing, coupled with Moses' eventual acceptance, he would endure countless grievous hardships, most of which likely were never recorded. Being essentially thrown out of the good life of yesterday and living with the animals of today would be easy compared to shepherding God's people. Oh the good ole days; sweltering days and cold nights with nothing but the animals and other critters. How easily Moses could slip back into longing for the obscurity of herding sheep.

Consider the fundamentals of life in Moses' day. Food, clothing, and shelter. Moving a massive group of some 600,000 men, plus women, children, and livestock, from a society where their needs were, to some extent, "provided"[33] to a society where they were responsible for meeting their own needs was a difficult task. Who would provide the food? What about the clothing and shelter? Besides, recall that this idea of telling Pharaoh "I am who I am" sent me, coupled with working what for all practical purposes appeared only as a few magic tricks, had failed miserably on all attempts but the last.[34] In fact, Moses' efforts would only make matters worse.

---

[33] Recall that the taskmasters (modern day police) initially gave the Israelites straw for brick building and subsequently it is inferred that the Egyptian government met the basic needs of their slaves, albeit very basic and despite the fact that the Israelites likely grew it, made it, and built it themselves.

[34] Of course, it is worth noting that God caused Pharaoh to respond adversely to Moses' request to free God's people. Again, we apparently need not understand.

It was not important that Moses understood the why, or even the how. He need only understand the fundamentals of the what, and obey. Such seems to be the life of the chosen. Here is what you are to do. Now, go for it. Of course, the problem arises when we allow the why to trump the how, and the how to trump the what, and in so doing, allow our frustration to negate the what, disobeying altogether.

God told Moses to go forth. Just go. "Go to Pharaoh and tell him to free my people." That was the initial charge God established. Nothing else. Perhaps more often than not, this is what we are told. Go. Despite that you think you are unprepared, go. Despite that you feel unworthy, go. Despite that you think you are a nobody, go. Despite that society thinks you will never amount to much, go. Despite all, go. Where there is God, there is a way, and for those honoring a call, the only way is his way. Obedience must always trump understanding.

To somewhat digress, is it not interesting the manner in which the text states that God was aware of the affliction of his people in Egypt, of the evil acts brought upon them by their taskmasters? God said, "So, I have come down to deliver them..." (Exodus 3:8) In context, it almost appears lackadaisical on God's part. "Yea, well I saw what was going on, so I decided I had better go down to give them a hand." What?! After 430 years you finally realized how your people were being treated? Remember that one of God's own orchestrated leaders got the Israelites in this situation in the first place when they sold out to the government. Albeit initially led by a God-fearing government leader at the time (Joseph), selling out to the government would become the precursor to the downfall of God's people, a point worth remembering.

The more excuses Moses offered to God's calling, the more God pressed. The more Moses waivered, the more steadfast God became, to the point that "the anger of the Lord burned against Moses" (Exodus 4:14) for his reluctance to go. Of course, this runs counter to our fairy tale wishes that God is all patient. Indeed, he is patient in many, many things, but at least in this case, he was not. "I said go; now go, and here, take this stick with you. I will teach you what you are to do." (cf. 15) Not, I have taught you what you are to do, rather, I will teach you what you are to do—*future tense*. What would have happened had God not applied this pressure? Had God not applied pressure in ways only he can, at least two things would have occurred. One, Moses would have disobeyed God, sinning in the process, and two, Moses' life would have spun out of control in a sea of doubt and ambiguity, always second guessing his reluctance to go. On the good days, his excuses for not accepting God's call would sound justified, and on other days his excuses would drive him to the brink of insanity. In the end, however, his countless attempts to rationalize God's call away would never rise above simply being an excuse, even to himself.

Late at night, again with his sheep, the stars, and the solitude of his thoughts, Moses would have pondered his decision. And as the days and nights grew into weeks, months, and years he would wrestle with that call, that divine yearning that could have been placed only by God himself. Nonetheless for Moses, the cool evening and beautiful sunset coupled with the comfort of the known, the sheep and other animals... Ahhhhh, it felt good to be home. Besides who would care for the animals if Moses had heeded that call? After all, God created the sheep, too. Someone has to care for the sheep and other animals.

Eventually however, maybe years after choosing the path of what appeared to be least resistant, Moses would allow himself to ever so slightly quietly question the wisdom of his decision to remain behind, to return to the fields. And as he pondered his decision regarding God's purpose for his life, his reason for living, he would stare into the face of disobedience again and again. Was he caring for the sheep, or were the sheep caring for him? Still, despite his disobedience, God was providing for him, but Moses would never know the blessing, guised as pain and suffering, God had waiting for Moses. As Dr. Tony Evans inadvertently summed up disobedience, "If you are not ready to commit, *stop looking for a blessing.*"

Clockwise from Top
Daddy & Mama, 1960, at Boot Camp, Fort Benning, US Army

Daddy, sisters Suzanne & Sherrie, and me

Daddy, Mama, Sherrie, Suzanne & me

From Top
Brandon, Natalie, and me, 2007, Washington, DC

Daddy, Mama, Brandon, Natalie, my wife Robin, and me, 2013, at Brandon's
graduation from Recruit Training, Parris Island, USMC

Brandon, Natalie, Robin, and me, 2014, Christmas

Brandon & Natalie, 2015, Thanksgiving

Brandon, 2016

Natalie, 2016

Daddy & Mama

Daddy

It's not about You

It's not about you. And it's not about me. It's about our maker, God Almighty, the I AM; and he alone. God solidified this point in the life of Job more so than in the life of any other person mentioned in the Bible. In fact, after all these years we continue to dissect this poor man's life.

We analyze, re-analyze, and synthesize Job's life in an attempt to understand Job's handling of the crisis and, moreover, God's willingness to destroy a blameless man. Piece by piece we investigate his life, the blessings that were given, and the blessings that were taken. We analyze it. We synthesize our analyses. Then we start over. The poor man would be shocked if he knew how much effort we put into understanding his struggles. The rights, and the wrongs that were rights. The good, the bad, and the ugly. The sweet and the salty; the black and the white. The relationship between God's opinion of Job and his actions toward him could not come with more polarity at the human level; the relationship was completely inverse. "...Blameless, upright, fearing God, and turning away from evil." (Job 1:1 & 8) Nonetheless, Satan, "Have you considered my servant Job?" (v. 8) "All that he has is in your power..." (v. 12) Wow. And remember, as far as we can tell, this situation did not result from a specific call God placed on Job's life, outside of being a faithful servant at a deeper level. It was just another day.

Of course, puzzling is the fact that Satan did not have to ask to destroy Job. *God suggested it.* Who does this? Well, God; and apparently it did not bother him. We infer this because God not only suggested that Satan destroy Job once; he suggested it twice! (2:3) More importantly however, God immediately follows up his offering of Job to Satan in 2:3 by admitting that such "ruin" was "without cause." So, who is this god, one who establishes even Satan's path toward destruction of his own? In fact, the only mandate to Satan was that he spare his life. Nothing else, just spare his life. If this does not disturb you as a Christian, you may need to consider deepening your spiritual thought processes.

Only after what certainly appeared as years of turmoil and unrest did God finally respond to Job and call a cease to the destruction in his life. Yet, as if completely destroying Job was not enough, God completely runs over Job in chapters 38 and 39, destroying what remnants may have survived as infinitesimally small pieces of Job's self-esteem. Job is destroyed psychologically by God. Again. And after the lengthy tongue lashing, Job finally assembles enough courage to respectfully respond to God by saying "Behold, I am insignificant..." (40:4) Can you hear Job? Listen closely. His response is barely audible. Weak and down trotted without the energy to say much more. Yet, Job's humility did not suffice; God went at him again.

> Then the Lord answered Job out of the storm, and said,
> "Now gird up your loins like a man; *I will ask you, and you instruct me*. Will you really annul my judgement? Will you condemn me that you may be justified? (Job 40: 6-8, emphasis mine)

We get the point. But perhaps not. God continues several more minutes challenging Job. It is almost as if God is either, 1) upset with Job's handing of God's decision to destroy him, or 2) upset with himself for allowing Satan to "incite" him against Job, or strongly persuade him to rise up against Job. (*cf.* Job 2:3) Certainly we want to use caution that we do not infer more than is stated here, but regardless of God's reasoning, Job was again humiliated for no reason. Finally, God pauses and Job again musters the courage to again respond.

> I know thou canst do all things, and that no purpose of thine can be thwarted. Who is this that hides counsel without knowledge? Therefore, I have declared that which I did not understand, things too wonderful for me, which I did not know.... I repent in dust and ashes. (Job 42:2-6)

Words such as these can only be appreciated fully through the lens of the defeated, of the destroyed; through one who has had everything and now has nothing. Nothing left to give, nothing left to offer. Defeated. One who is spent, finished, and no more. Perhaps even a never has been. Perhaps borderline apathy, not necessarily love or hate. Job no longer had a position; he just existed. He was *just here*. But, if at no other point in Job's life, he now fully realized the most important lesson in life. His life was not about him; *it was about Him*. Job, coupled with his many successes, did not matter. In the end, Job said very, very little, but ironically, he said it all. *I am insignificant.*

It's about Him

It's not about you. This simple construct serves as our most fundamental stumbling block. In fact, for only one person in the history of mankind has this not been a stumbling block. It's not about you; and it's not about me. The idea runs counter to self, to who we are as sinners, or at least to who we have become since Adam and Eve ate of the forbidden fruit. It runs contrary to nearly everything we learn as a child into adulthood.

I played sports as a child and teenager. Football, softball, and tennis were my sports, and I was a pretty decent athlete, as I humbly recall. In some cases, I had practice and/or games for all three several times in any given week, but in every sport, there was always a winner and always a loser. You won; I lost. I won; you lost. We won the football game Friday night but lost the softball game Saturday. Then I won my singles match but lost the doubles match. Today, however, every kid is a winner. Every kid. They all receive trophies. They receive what amounts to participation trophies, or trophies for showing up, but what a dreadful precedence this establishes for kids.

We coddle them and stroke their already overly inflated self-esteems. We tell them they are the best at everything they attempt; every sport, every subject, every activity. Then they graduate from being number one in sports and other activities to their teenage years. There, we oh so gently encourage them through school as to not run the risk of harming their delicate little egos. We buy them high dollar prom dresses to wear one time; besides, how could we actually ask them to wear something that has already been worn. We buy them Polo, Ralph Lauren, Brooks Brothers, Hollister, American Eagle, and Abercrombie & Fitch. Heck, when my sisters and I were growing up, we wore so many ugly clothes from J.C. Penny that our parents should be investigated for child humiliation! Then again, in the seventh grade I graduated to the popular; I had arrived. Mama finally got me a pair of Levi's. Of course, they were hand-me-downs from someone a foot taller than me, but no one would know as long as I rolled up the bottoms and my sisters kept their large mouths closed. I was in the 7th grade at Blackshear Junior High School, and styling. They had that red tag on the back pocket with their iconic stitching. The funny thing was, of course, my paddlings at school hurt just as much in my new Levis as they did in my Plain Pockets from J.C. Penny's.

But now we buy our kids laptops, IPods, IPads, guns, four-wheelers, skateboards, wakeboards. And cars and trucks at 16, and sometimes 15, not so they can get to work, mind you; they *don't* work. When I graduated high school and began my freshman year in college, I had saved the equivalent of what would be $26,000 today, all from cutting grass at $5 a yard and picking tobacco for $20 a day. What a difference a generation makes. And oh, I am sorry; a few of my readers may not know what cutting grass is… you know, *landscaping*. We called it cuttin' grass then because it involved sweat.

Then as today's kids move into young adulthood we set them up in apartments and houses as they complete college and maybe graduate school, and enter the workforce for the first time with limited to no work ethic or communication skills. But remember; they are number one, and yes, life *is* about them. Their entire life we have set them up for success and in the process firmly placed them on a path to fail.

What if David had not recognized he was not the center of life when he faced Goliath? He was just a kid facing a hardened warrior. Certainly, he would have met death that day, if not before, and it would have been his head on the platter. But young David knew better. Through his trials with bears, lions, and other predators he had learned to depend wholly on God, and more importantly, *holy* on God. David knew before the fight the victory had been won. All he had to do was give the fight to the Lord. He knew as few others that life was about Him—at least today.

God's word is clearer on this single topic than with any other. Repeatedly we are told that life is not about us; not me, not you. In multiple ways, through multiple examples, we learn that life is about Him. Yet our sin nature wrestles with this construct more than any other. We resist. We fight. And we lose. And we repeat the process hopelessly expecting a different outcome.

We long to be in control of everything associated with our lives, and that of others. No matter how fierce the fight, no matter how long the fight, we hang in there to the bitter end clawing our way toward our position, despite knowing many of the consequences of doing so before the fight begins.

Like us, Jonah was adamant. He would have his way no matter the costs. God could direct, instruct, and lead all he wanted; Jonah was *not* going to Nineveh. The Assyrians could enjoy hell as far as Jonah was concerned. Only in the belly of a fish did Jonah begin to accept that life was not about him, but Him. Conversely, Abraham walked his son to his grave. He fought against his own flesh, but his lack of understanding never trumped his position in God's hierarchy.

The disciples and other followers heeded the call to follow Jesus and his teachings, and they suffered immensely for that decision. Peter was crucified. So were others. But God chose them, and each paid a dreadful price for following him, with nearly all of these followers experiencing great suffering and pain. Yet they obeyed. Perhaps more often than not, they did not understand. Their walks were lonely; their walks were arduous. But they learned ultimately that their circumstances should never dictate their theology. Even Paul, a great man we have neglected to discuss here, his life was not about himself, nor was Peter's life, and so it was with every follower of Christ, including Judas. All disciples, apostles, and other followers would eventually learn the misgivings of being self-serving.

Over and over Moses would approach Pharaoh with vigor in an attempt to have the Israelites released from bondage as slaves to a wicked government that had held them captive for 430 years. As God directed, Moses approached Pharaoh, and only with exception of the last attempt, God hardened Pharaoh's heart such that he would not release the people; and with each attempt God's sole purpose was to demonstrate to the Israelites and Egyptians that he and he alone, was God. "So, that you will know that I am your God." It was not about them. It was not about Moses. It was about Him.

Such is our struggle. It is personal. Just you. Just God. And our struggle. Our struggle, that desire to forfeit our will for ourselves to follow God into the unknown, the abyss, into an unquantifiable and unexplainable uncertainty that only he can control. Coupled with our fight to succeed on our terms against his will, our life becomes unrecognizable, a mere fragment of what it was when we were in control. And the uncertainty mounts. Oh, it begins simple enough; seeking his will on a couple of issues, yet moving toward the contrary of not what we believe is best but what we want. We yield here and there on a few small things, of course, Besides, we have to show some cooperation. He is our maker, after all. Perhaps at least we should show up. So, we continue haphazardly yielding to the small things in life, but unknown to us we are leaving an ever-increasing mountain of disobedience by way of casual resistance. We move through life, through marriage, children, and careers, and through it all we secretly struggle with unfulfilled calls he placed on our lives years ago, and yesterday. Like Jonah, we fight, and we resist. And before we realize what is happening, our mountain crashes down upon us with no mercy as a reminder that life is indeed not about us; it is about Him.

Herbert M Barber, Jr, PhD, PhD

Herbert M Barber, Jr, PhD, PhD

When the Leader becomes the Servant

Leadership has remained a buzz word in society for several years. Today Americans are so desperate for authentic leadership that they annually pay millions of dollars to self-proclaimed leadership "experts." In fact, one of the most well-known Christian speakers on leadership today has never led.

L eadership. We manage entities; we lead people. We manage companies; we lead people. We manage projects and processes; we lead people. As one well-versed in systems engineering[35] and one fairly well versed in organizational learning,[36] but certainly not an expert on leadership, I contend

---

[35] At its core, systems engineering is a multi-disciplined area of engineering that centers on the design and management of complex engineering systems over their life cycles, which includes but is not limited to people and processes.

[36] Though somewhat a rudimentary definition of organizational learning, organizational learning centers on the complex relationships associated with

that leadership is innate, a spiritual gift God grants a handful of persons upon their acceptance of Christ as their personal Savior. As such, I contend that authentic leadership cannot be taught, despite the best efforts of leadership gurus. For those Christians who have the spiritual gift of leadership, it can be perfected through study and practice, and further study and practice, but it cannot be taught, and thus, it cannot be learned. One is a leader, or he is not.

In theory, leadership is a complex construct; in reality, it is an ambiguous construct that researchers have yet to fully operationalize as a variable. Thus, leadership is very difficult to quantifiably measure. Nonetheless, everyone seems to want to lead today, to stand out from the crowd, to be number one. Very few want to serve. It reminds me of the younger college graduates we have hired in the past. They have completed college and graduate school. They have worked hard, and now they are ready to set the world on fire, ready to solve the world's hunger problem. There is only one problem: They don't know how to grow the garden. Most want a position, not a job. They want the

---

social units, including but not limited to, their learning, development, and growth individually and collectively.

prestige that comes with the position without the effort mandated by the job. They want the title but not the work linked to the title. They want to lead, not to serve. I guess Thomas Edison was right. "Opportunity is missed by most people because it is dressed in overalls and looks like work."

It brings to mind a young man we hired against our better judgment. I had him as a student in an undergraduate course I taught one night a week as an adjunct at Georgia Southern University. On a return trip from Atlanta I passed through the town in which he was working and called him, just to check on him. "Now, you are handling everything for us, aren't you?" I asked. "Oh, yes sir." "Well," I said, "I just wanted to make sure you are there giving our client what he is paying for, you know. I mean, you need to be on site. I don't want you kicked back in the hotel not working." "Oh, no sir, Dr. Barber. I would never be in the hotel when I was supposed to be working." And, with that I hung up, then placed my business card on the window of his truck—at the hotel.

Not too many years ago we managed entity and person, only to eventually rule entity and person with an iron fist, right up until people offered significant resistance through the development of unions, organizations originally structured for the good of the people, the workers. But what happens when the leader becomes the servant? What happens when the leader is no longer served, but serves? Does he still garner the same level of respect? Or any respect at all? He was working on the company side; now he works on the union side. Should he lead by following, follow by leading, or neither? Conversely, what happens when the servant becomes the leader, when he moves from the union to the company, so to speak? What happens when the servant no longer serves but is served? Does he garner a higher level of respect, or is he always seen only as the servant? Does his stored litany of experience and knowledge of serving serve him well as leader? Or does he too eventually fail, likely overtaken by self.

Though my father has never seen himself as a leader, per se, he is a gifted leader. No, he never managed a large organization. His name has never appeared with the rich and famous in our hometown, nor has he ever been listed on Forbes 400. I do not even recall his name being outside his office door, and if it was, he certainly never put it there. But he is a leader, nonetheless.

To this day, Daddy leads through serving. He is never out front; rather, he is in back where the work occurs, but in ways still unknown to me, it puts him out front. How could one who has so little to say, say so much? Daddy is, in fact, the quintessential picture of what has been coined, servant-leader, one who leads by serving, or by example for the greater good of others.[37] It is a gift, a spiritual gift. And what a powerful impact he makes on those who know him, professionally and personally, for to know him is to model him.

Like Daddy, Mr. Kirkland was a man of few words, a quiet man. As a teenager, he appeared to me to be in his mid-100s, likely even older. I knew little of him, though he lived a couple houses down. Then again, how could I really know him; I rarely saw him, and when I did, he rarely spoke. Like I said, he was in his mid-100s. He simply stood with Daddy as the two non-talkers watched me shoot basketball in the yard, likely while rambling about my latest activities, or trying to get out of splitting wood that afternoon. Yet, without fail, every time I saw Mr. Kirkland, he posed one simple question, one that pierced the air, demanding

---

[37] Though servant leadership has been traced back centuries, Robert Greenleaf is credited for coining the actual term in 1970, as well as giving the term formal definition. In brief, Greenleaf sought to define a better method for managing organizations than through the traditionally accepted dictatorial management methods he experienced in business and industry. Additional information regarding Greenleaf and servant leadership is readily available through multiple mediums, including the *Robert K. Greenleaf Center for Servant Leadership*.

a definitive dichotomous response, either yes, or no. "Have you got your ticket?" Do you have your ticket? Have you accepted Christ as your Savior? If today was your last day, do you know for certain you would spend eternity in heaven? Would you sit at the feet of the one who served, or the one who longs to be served? Funny how Mr. Kirkland led while essentially saying nothing. A single sentence; an influential ministry. Perhaps Adrian Rogers summed up Mr. Kirkland's message best. "I wouldn't trust the best fifteen minutes I ever lived to get me into heaven."

Jesus was a servant-leader. Like Daddy, he led by serving— the antithesis of what most consider as leadership today. He remained in the background, in the background where the only recognition is unrecognized on earth. And what an impact. Over two thousand years later we still use Jesus as the standard through which we model behavior. What would Jesus do, they say. Well, in our case today, likely not what we are doing.

His walk to Calvary was horrific. It was humiliating and painful, more grueling, physically, emotionally, psychologically, and spiritually than we shutter to envision, or care to describe. The anguish was overwhelming. He had been betrayed, not only by Judas, mind you. Judas did the deed, but they all fled. So, there is no need to point fingers here; they all deceived him.

Jesus was cheated, just as the pending solidity of sin was readied for his shoulders. He stood alone; he stood rejected, lonely, and dejected as a broken fragment of a man. But he remained steadfast to his call, to who he was, and to the god who called him, God the Father. And he did so solely on our behalf, for those times of yesterday that you hated, and those times you will hate tomorrow, for those decisions you knew would harm others, but you made anyway, and for those things you did with callous and mischief, guised with a chuckle. For those things you did, and those things I did, and for those things we will do, he hung, spent. Hanging, chocking, gasping, and bleeding with his pending death chocking out the oxygen like a heavy fog, he cried, "ELI, ELI, LAMA SABACHTHANI?" "My God, My God, why have You forsaken Me?" (Matthew 27:46; as earlier quoted by David in Psalms 22:1). There is no better example of servant leadership, friend. He died a vicious death; I live eternally.

Where would we be had Jesus not served, had the leader not become the servant? Had he not endured death on the cross? What if he came to earth as the child of a virgin birth and chose his own path? No time spent in the synagogue learning, let alone teaching. None of his days spent modeling God in his life as he went about his day. No healings, no miracles, and no followers; just one of the boys. "Oh, these bunch of grumbling people make me sick. Can they do nothing for themselves? I think I'll take some time off, maybe hang out with the boys at the beach a few days." Remember, if we believe that Jesus was fully man, then he was *fully* man, meaning that he had within him the power to choose otherwise. Thus, he had the power to choose to not endure the cross, forcing mankind to live under the law forever, which in turn, would likely mean eternal damnation for most of us. Fortunately, however, Jesus was not only fully man during his tenure on earth, he was also *fully* God.

Along with Jesus, perhaps the servants exemplifying God most in their lives who eventually became great leaders were Joseph and Moses. If we contrast these men of God against one another, and we are completely honest, one led God's people into captivity, and one lead God's people out of captivity. Ironically, however, both saved God's people.

Both leaders began life as pampered children, one as the spoiled youngest of a relatively successful man of God, and one as the spoiled child in the house of Pharaoh. Both were special, and likely both knew they were. Moses certainly was; after all, he lived in the house of the king! And as for Joseph, well Joseph let us know that he was special; he told his father and brothers as much when he implied that they would one day bow to him.

Likely both had the best of everything; the best slingshots, the coolest of everything. They hung out with the Jones' kids down the street, the upper crust in the neighborhood, or at least those who thought they were. They both likely earned the best educations money could provide. Dummies, they were not. They were intelligent, and they likely hung around relatively intelligent people, deepening their knowledge base. To a large extent, both had grown used to being pampered, to being served. Yet both would endure grievous hardships prior to assuming their formal roles as leader—as servants. One would spend over a decade with lofty titles such as pit dweller, slave, servant, adulterer, and prisoner. And as for this other great man of God? Oh, he would simply be known as murderer, or perhaps to those who really hated him, killer—before he then spent forty years with the title of goat herder, shepherd, and keeper of the flock.

Both would lead, but before they led, both would serve. And they would serve not at the Ritz Carlton in Cairo, but in the filth of the fields and prisons. They would do as they were instructed. They would not question their role in society, not aloud anyway. They were at the bottom, and they knew they were at the bottom. Besides, questioning why they were at the bottom could only serve so many purposes, few of which were positive.

Joseph's journey to leadership would be nearly intolerable. Hanging out in the pit for a few hours was like a walk in the park compared to how the balance of the next thirteen years of leadership training would go. God may have given him the gift of leadership, but knocking down the rough edges so the gift was usable would not come without a cost, for Joseph would never be the leader God needed with the gift alone. He needed a little face time with rejection, disappointment, and loneliness. He needed to experience the harsh reality of being sold into slavery as if he was nothing, the one who was "no more," as his life did not matter. He needed to experience a life of deep pain and suffering, a life of being accused of something he did not do while his accuser went fancy-free. He needed to experience life without life, where only the prison walls hear your pleas for the truth to be known.

Though Moses' course in leadership would appear more tolerable, it would be no less miserable. Nor would it last only a decade or so. No, the course God developed for Moses was one that would drag on for decades, *four decades*, in fact, taking him into what would be for me, the pits of boredom. Just hanging out with the animals, miserable with his thoughts, only there at the mercy of his father-in-law. Did he regret killing the Egyptian? Maybe today. Maybe not tomorrow. But he had forty years to contemplate the decision that led to his circumstances. Perhaps today he would be regretful and tomorrow he would wish he had killed more. They were destroying good, hard-working people, God's people, benefiting from the sweats of their brow, similar to what we have in the US today. They deserved to be put in their place. Then again, it wasn't Moses' place to render such decisions, especially those necessitating retribution. Joseph's place. Yours. Or mine.

Herbert M Barber, Jr, PhD, PhD

Bring on the Rain

Both Joseph and Moses would survive God's program on leadership, and moreover, his lessons on significance. Joseph's program would require less time, but the coursework would be concentrated, grueling, and more intense. Moses' program would be long suffering; he would attend graduate school for many, many years with no graduation date in mind, toiling away with his studies. But both would become authorities on what it really meant to be significant.

*I*n the interim, they would be students in the toughest graduate program in the world, those orchestrated and implemented by God himself. God would develop their programs; every trial, every defeat, and every victory, few as they were. And he alone would develop the rubric and do the scoring. So the rain would fall. And it would fall without mercy, and without end, and just when Joseph and Moses thought they could take no more rain, thunder and lightning would begin pelting them from out of nowhere as they cowered in a grief masked only with the slightest of hope that God may possibly deliver them from the storm someday.

They would weather the storm until God decided it was time to move to the next storm. And just as they came up for air, they would find themselves bombarded by the next storm; this time, a storm much worse than the previous. Any victories of yesterday's storms would quickly fade as they realized the frailties of their strengths today. And through their increasing weaknesses they would only then find themselves back at the feet of God, begging not for understanding, but mercy. And the storm would continue.

Such is life for those whom God has placed difficult calls. "You want to be significant? This is what I consider significant." Above all else, as Jesus instructed the scribe, "You shall love the Lord your God with all your heart; and with all your soul, and with all your mind, and with all your strength." (Mark 12:30) And if you do, "You will have no other gods before me." (*cf.* Exodus 20:3) Thus, to become significant, one must become insignificant (*cf.* Job 40:4, Corinthians 4:5, Mark 10:44, and multiple other verses). "If anyone wants to be first, he shall be last of all, *and servant of all.*" (Mark 9:35; emphasis mine)

In so doing, we must realize the significance of being insignificant, realizing that our secular accomplishments mean nothing without God, and thus, nothing eternally. Think about that; surely this is something many deeply committed Christians have pondered as by no means is this concept unique. We hear it every Sunday in the few churches left who still use God's word as the basis for study and worship. Unfortunately, we never give the concept its due consideration. We hear brush over it as trivial knowledge for the new Christian.

Nearly every accomplishment on earth for which we so desperately toil means nothing. The prestigious positions that come with our careers, the incomes we slave to earn, our nice houses, cars, boats, and other toys. Our education, expertise, and notoriety. Those moments our world does revolve around us. Nothing. These accomplishments mean nothing without God. Yet we readily pursue the insignificant as though it were our god, right up until they become our god. We should just count our blessings when God doesn't use our accomplishments against us—because he does.

And for those who beg to differ, those who mouth words on Sunday morning only to give the appearance they too want God to use them in a powerful and mighty way as he did Joseph, Moses, Noah, Paul, David, and a host of others, woe to you. "No matter what it takes, God, use me. Mold me and make me, humbly I pray. Have thine own way, Lord; have thine own way." Careful what you wish for, friend, or in this case, that for which you pray. He may give you just that, and trust me; you do not want that which you are asking. Oh, you want a few of the results associated with what you are asking. Maybe we all do, but you by no means want to endure the graduate program God will orchestrate to get you there. No. No, you don't.

The unfortunate irony, of course, is that we know not what we ask. We don't know what we don't know, and until we know, we don't know. Five academic degrees coupled with a little experience taught me that! But do not allow the simplicity of the sentence structure nor its grammatical simplicity lead you to scoff or become derisive. The statement is profound. If you seek God with all of your being, not merely accept him as your Savior and show up on Sunday mornings, but you earnestly lay down your life to seek and yield to his will regardless of immeasurable costs, your life very likely will be shattered beyond recognition. And I can suggest that emphatically.

Some twenty years ago I ignorantly pled with God to use me, to take me to the pit so just perhaps, one day he could use me. Earnestly, I prayed, day after day as I traveled for work and graduate school. And with the passing of several years, I had long forgotten that I had spent weeks in earnest prayer that God would profoundly shape me into his vessel. Unfortunately, however, he had not. He remembered every hour I had spent on the highways and in the airways with little to do but earnestly pray. And after more than a decade of walking along the fringes of hell on earth, no; no, I now realize I had no idea what I was asking, for the rain would fall, and the lightning would strike. And the storms would worsen.

After more than a decade of weathering storms orchestrated by God that keep me on my knees, I would never request such from my maker again. Never. Then again, nor would I give you anything for the storms. I am but a fragment of the man I was, now barely recognizable. Weathered and worn, rejected and dejected. Still a long way from usable perhaps, but barely recognizable nonetheless. "...I considered all my activities which my hands had done and the labor which I had exerted, and behold all was vanity and striving after wind..." (Ecclesiastes 2:11) As John Wesley surmised, "When I was young I was sure of everything; in a few years, having been mistaken a thousand times, I was not half so sure of most things as I was before. At present, I am hardly sure of anything but what God has revealed to me."

Herbert M Barber, Jr, PhD, PhD

Rejecting the Genuine; accepting the Spurious

"When you reject the genuine, you are wide open for the spurious." I wish I could credit myself for this statement as it says so much about where most of us stand in our Christian walks, but these words were spoken by the great theologian, Dr. J. Vernon McGee.

Stay with me as we talk shop a minute... In statistics, the term *spurious* refers to a phenomenon that exhibits quantitative characteristics tending to suggest that two or more events, such as constructs, variables, relationships, or the like, are causal, meaning that at least one independent event quantitatively causes a dependent event, while any noted causes are in fact merely derivatives of unrelated events altogether, or what we commonly refer to as confounding events or variables.

In economics, or econometrics in this case, we typically use observational data to develop causal relationships. For example, we may use the gross domestic product (GDP) of a nation coupled with other variables, say some other development ratio, to model and project variables such as energy demand. Of course, in this example, we may be able to argue that any causal relationship here is also bi-directional, but such is not our worry as this is not our topic of concern, today. However, to stay with our discussion defining spurious, what if we determined using, say Granger-causality,[38] that there also was a causal relationship between bottled water sales in the US and energy demand? Could we conclude that an increase in bottled water sales causes an increase in US energy demand? Likely not, no more than we could conclude that an increase in energy demand causes an increase in bottled water sales. "Bottled water sales" here is a confounding variable, and at the very best, a latent variable, as any increases in both bottled water sales and energy demand may be due to extreme weather conditions across the US. Thus, the relationship

---

[38] For what it is worth in this discussion, which is to say, nothing, Granger-causality is a statistical technique for determining whether a particular time series model can forecast another time series. Assuming the data are robust and relatively stable, the technique is a sound technique for examining causality, as well as whether such relationships are non-directional, uni-directional, or bi-directional.

is spurious; bottled water sales and energy demand likely are independent of one another in terms of causality. In the end, causal relationships are derivatives of how their respective constructs were operationalized—or in lay terms, established.

The fundamental problem in Christian circles today is that we accept the spurious and reject the genuine, and in so doing open ourselves to the spurious becoming our truth. Thus, the truth as we see it is now a subjective relative truth, at best. Perhaps the easiest way to view this paradox is by considering the relationship between happiness and joy. By definition, happiness can parallel joy, but happiness is not synonymous with joy; happiness and joy are not one in the same. By no means was Paul happy to be in prison; nonetheless, he was joyful. But let's take this idea of spurious further.

Most Christians today are more interested in what they want to know about God than they are in actually knowing God. As such, we are interested in being served by him than in serving him. What can he do for me? We say we want to know him, but do we? Do we really want to know God for who he is, or only for who we want him to be? Our response defines our relationship with him, and our actions define our response.

For example, most churches today offer nothing but what they see as God's goodness; the baby in Bethlehem, a kind, gentle God who just wants to cradle and love you. It is often reflective in churches caught up in not only charismatic movements, but churches who no longer use expository means of studying scripture, opting rather to use topical methods where picking and choosing a verse here and there that depicts God's goodness is viewed more favorable by pulpiteers and pew warmers, alike.

And the people flock to these church services by the thousands. In fact, by subjective examination, which is to say there may be no scientific merit to this whatsoever, it appears that churches who preach God's goodness are exploding with holy rollers while backwoods, Bible-thumping churches where toe-stepping is preferred to side-stepping are decreasing with each passing generation of saints. "You want success? You can have it. You want riches? You can have that, too. The god we serve is a good god. He is here for you, brother!" While these statements may be true, they are not biblically sound, and they are not biblically sound because they present only partial scriptural truths; and as we have learned, it is impossible for a partial truth to rise above being anything but a complete lie.

So, we pray for God's goodness, perhaps for success, and he blesses us with it, only to then realize that success is not what we thought, as with much success comes much heartache. As they say, "Show me one thousand men who can handle adversity, and I will show you one man who can handle success."

Well, then maybe riches will do the trick. So, we pray for riches, maybe a lot of fortune, and he blesses us with riches. Everywhere we go, we are recognized as an infamous leader in our fields of useless infinitive knowledge. And we have riches to blow as if there is no tomorrow. Apparently, we are back to success, and "God is good; he is so good! Just look how he has blessed me!" Unfortunately, with the passing of time we realize that we have accepted the spurious for the genuine. In fact, we have accepted the spurious *as* the genuine. We worshipped the provisions while negating the provider. But we worked hard; we did our part. Only if we too had recognized as the writer of Ecclesiastes did, that "All a man's labor is for his mouth and the appetite is not satisfied." (6:7)

Only following much calamity do we finally realize that most of our deep-seated desires in life are merely senseless follies for the foolhardy. No, the spurious has not satisfied. We received the desires of our hearts and realized they were but dust. We had honored God with our lips, but our hearts were far from him, as we worshipped in vain, teaching the doctrines of men. (*cf.* Mark 7:6-7)

Hopefully we need no further evidence of these type misnomers in our lives. After all, we live with them daily. Every day we seek some desire, some goal, some accomplishment or recognition. And for many of us, the only thing running more deeply than our desires are our wills. We seek them, we sacrifice everything, we attain them, and we realize that which we have sought, while substantial, is without lasting merit. We accepted the spurious as the genuine, and it did not satisfy. What does it profit us to negate the will of our father with triumphs of our own? More pointedly, "...what does it profit a man to gain the whole world, and forfeit his soul?" (Mark 8:36)

Subsequently, perhaps it can be argued that the real worth of a man can be derived through his uncanny ability to hold loosely the things of which he most desires. God giveth, and God taketh. It is his to give; and it is his to take. I know of no man who knows this better than, again, our friend Job. God blessed him mightily with creature comforts, and in an instance they were gone. Taken. No more. God gave, and God took. And the spurious became dust. Yet foolishly we fight to hang on to the dust we have collected so we too can be significant. Our toys, our businesses, our intellect.

The god we want him to be. The spurious that overtakes the genuine. He closes the door, even slams it, yet we remain there banging. And while we often know that which we desire is but spurious, we seek it with an unparalleled will where our defiant attempt toward attainment says more about us than the spurious we so feverishly seek. Oh, how unwise the wise become when we allow our will to supersede his will. How God must chuckle at the folly of our wisdom, "Because the foolishness of God is wiser than men..." (1 Corinthians 1:25) Rejecting the genuine; accepting the spurious. But, *bang on, brother!*

Herbert M Barber, Jr, PhD, PhD

Lessons from the Pit

Resisting life's struggles comes naturally to us, but doing so often is one of the most damming ways we can respond in terms of spiritual growth. The pit, as Joseph was in literally for a while and figuratively for several years, is a daunting place to reside, even for short stays. It is demanding, denigrating, demeaning, and destructive; and it will destroy you if you respond incorrectly.

A bove all, remember, God controls the pit. He controls when you enter the pit, and when you leave the pit. He controls your stay in its entirety. The length of the stay, the quality of the stay, and the cost of the stay. And make no mistake about it; the cost of your stay in the pit will be daunting. Well, do you want significance? It comes not by walking the fringes of the pit, but through the pit.

Nothing is cheap in the pit. You are dealing with our maker, remember, and he does not skimp on quality. You will receive more than your money's worth. In fact, what you receive in the pit will be of unparalleled quality, something you never forget. However, there is no definitive method for determining what characteristics and events will comprise your pit, assuming you enter the pit.

As for my pit, my pit was arduous, one that lasted over a decade, one that lasts until this day, and one that will likely never end. Coupled with numerous other simultaneous struggles in the pit, any one of which would have made the strongest Christian cower, I was simultaneously and inadvertently forced to delve into the dark world of psychopathy. And for even the discerning Christian, dealing with a psychopath is unlike dealing with any other creature God placed on earth, for to deal with a psychopath is to come face to face with darkness in its rawest form—every day. And the day after that. So, weakly analogous to the day they turned off the lights deep inside Mammoth Cave, Kentucky on me as a child, you learn to shuffle through life slowly with keen insight and caution taken with every movement lest you be overtaken by the darkness.

To involuntarily or voluntarily open the door to a psychopath is to woefully open the door to Satan—Lucifer, Beelzebub, the Power of Darkness, the Father of Lies, the Ruler of Darkness, the Serpent, the Tempter, the Thief, the Accuser, the Adversary, the Apollyon, the Great Fiery Red Dragon, the Man of Sin, the Enemy, the Angel of the Abyss, and the permanent Angel of the Bottomless Pit. (*cf.* Revelation 9:11. 1 Peter 5:8. Luke 11:15, Revelation 12:3, Isaiah 14:12, 2 Thessalonians 2:3-4, Colossians 1:13, and Matthew 4:13, for starters) And even synthesized as noted, this description does not begin to describe the blanket of darkness that covers your life when a psychopath places you in their crosshair.

Psychopaths are neither necessarily hyper-intelligent nor obtuse, but they are relentless in every endeavor they undertake. Having notable characteristics of Satan himself, coupled with this relentless defiant nature, their sole objective is to completely control their victims by destroying them so they, themselves, may be elevated. Cloaked by charm and charisma, engulfed with evil, and birthed in hell, a psychopath has no conscious. Subsequently, he has not the human capacity to empathize, let alone love.[39] Everything about him is demonic and evil, and the human being is powerless against him. To deal with a psychopath is to deal with a darkness that reeks of hell, and a darkness that can only be found through Satan.

A psychopath is a master manipulator. He moves about life without fear of repercussion, without fear of harm befalling him, breaking laws and social norms that normal people never entertain, all while accusing others of evils only he himself commits. He is a user and abuser of people, a master deceiver with every breath. He views humans as puppets, as property, there to be exploited for his purposes so he can reign supremely. Yes, similarly to the anti-Christ. His victims, he stalks. He plans, he plots, and he schemes. He lies and he cheats. And he bums, literally, seeking that which is not his.

---

[39] For reference, refer to every scholar, researcher, and clinician who serve as experts on psychopathy; there is no disagreement in the scientific literature or in clinical practice as to the psychopath's inability to genuinely empathize, love, or care for mankind in any form. However, the psychopath is a master at mimicking emotions of others; thus, they very effectively give the appearance of empathy and love to their family, children, friends, colleagues, and strangers.

He is obsessively boisterous, often even obnoxious. But he is very patient as he lies in wait for his next ambush. And just when you think his evil rants and subsequent triumphs have subsided, he pounces with a vengeance that can only be sourced through hell itself, for, after all, the psychopath answers directly to Lucifer, and only Lucifer. Literally. Yes, Lucifer. Satan.

With cold blank stares, one of the psychopaths who abused my family leveraged his power as a cop to manipulate *his* people— other cops, district attorneys, and judges—to control us, to destroy us, personally and professionally. And his control over people hath no equal. Outside of God Almighty, neither does Satan's. But make no mistake about it; a psychopath is not sick, nor is he mentally unstable, unfit, or disturbed. He is not socially inept. He is evil. And nothing else. He is *of Satan*. And if you cross him, you will lose. Hear me, for every step you gain, you will lose ninety-nine. As for me, however, "...[my] struggle is not against flesh and blood, but against the rulers, against the powers, against the world forces of this darkness, against the spiritual forces of wickedness in the heavenly places." (Ephesians. 6:12)

It is indeed against the darkness of this world that I fight. The darkness I fight is just clothed in human form. Refer back to

Genesis 6:4 I referenced earlier in our discussion regarding the evils associated with the days of Noah; and hear my words with an unbiased mind regarding the origins of the modern-day psychopath. Only then will you begin to grasp an infinitely small spec of the darkness that comes when you cross paths with a one of Lucifer's own, the psychopath, and the origin of my adversaries.

> The Nephilim [those who have fallen[40]] were on the earth in those days, <u>and also afterward</u>, when the sons of God came in to the daughters of men, and they bore children to them [creating the Elioud race]. Those were the mighty men who were of old, men of renown. (Genesis 6:4; commentary and emphasis mine)

So through fallen angels, the Nephilim, darkness fell across the earth in the days of Noah. And this darkness, or evil, increased as the Nephilim procreated with human women, creating a separate race of beings called Elioud, a race of sub-humans God described as one having "every intent of the thoughts of his heart [of] only evil continually." (Genesis 6:5, commentary mine)

---

[40] Geerts, L. (n.d.), as noted in Giants, Nephilim, and Anakim.

So, the earth was "filled with violence" (Genesis 6:11 and 6:13) and "corrupt," (Genesis 6:12) so much so that God said, "the end of flesh is before me... and behold, I am about to destroy them with the earth." (Genesis 6:13) Stay with me; remember this is in Noah's day, and we are investigating the origins of the psychopath, those demonic beings that roam the earth today... So not only was God going to destroy this wickedness, he was going to do so using the very thing, ie, earth, he had given them to enjoy (Hence, the flood). Further, he would use what he considered "good" (*cf.* Genesis 1) to destroy what he considered evil.

Of course, we would have expected the Nephilim and Elioud to have been destroyed during the flood, right? As such, this idea presents a quandary. For example, in Genesis 6:19, God instructs Noah to take "every living thing of all flesh," "two of every kind into the ark," "keeping them alive," with those taken being "male and female." So, did Noah consider the Nephilim and Elioud, evil as they were, part of "every living thing of all flesh," or did he consider them part of the "them" God referred to in Genesis 6:13, that which was to be completely destroyed? In other words, did Noah load these beings on the ark, or leave them for death?

God's word gives no definitive answer here. However, one argument to these beings surviving the Genesis flood is found in the book of Jubilees,[41] an ancient Jewish text not considered canonical within most Protestant denominations, but with writings worth consideration nonetheless. Jubilees maintains that God allowed ten percent of this race to temporarily circumvent Tartarus (presumably a place analogous to, or associated with, hell) to attempt to lead humanity spiritually astray in the future (Recall that we also are told in Genesis 6:4, noted above, that the Nephilim would roam earth *after the flood*, as well; hence the phrase, "and also afterward.").

Let the tenth part of them remain before him, and let nine parts descend into the place of condemnation. (Jubilees 10:9)

Thus, these beings would still roam earth today. However, for those who prefer to completely discount Jubilees, as the book is

---

[41] The book of Jubilees, Enoch, and similar books are not considered canonical, and I am not in a position to suggest such in either regard. But remember, men determined which books would be included, and what books would not be included, in the Christian Bible. However, ancient books such as these have the potential to shed great historical depth to topics under discussion and, thus, should never be discounted without tremendous investigation, prayer, and discernment.

not canonical, as well as that noted in Genesis 6:4 regarding the beings roaming the earth after the flood, which is canonical, refer to Numbers 13, specifically Numbers 13:28, forward. Here we again find that the Nephilim, also known as the sons of Anak (v. 33), are on earth—even after the Genesis flood. Thus, we find the Nephilim and Elioud roaming the earth both "pre-flood" and "post-flood,"[42] whether by surviving the flood or through additional procreation between fallen angels and womankind.

Still skeptical? Then, tell me why the spies noted in Numbers 13, those who scouted the Land of Canaan, the exact land God was giving his people, (*cf.* Numbers 13-14) returned terrified as scurrying "grasshoppers" when they saw "the Nephilim" living in the land. (*cf.* Numbers 13:33) Was Caleb and his team of bandits merely afraid of mortal men, men whom they knew God could easily overtake? Were they afraid of mere flesh and blood? Hardly. They immediately recognized their struggle to overtake the land. Their struggle was against the "rulers, against the powers, against the world forces of this darkness" and "spiritual forces." (Ephesians 6:12)

---

[42] Hodge, B. (208). Who were the Nephilim. Answers in Genesis. Also refer to Deuteronomy 2 for reference to the "sons of Anak," beings directly linked to the Nephilim, as well.

These beings were, and are, engulfed with satanic endeavors, and they roam earth, seeking to destroy man. But let us operationalize this construct even further. Who radiates darkness in our modern world? The psychopath, and lest Satan himself, he hath no equal. With near one hundred percent probability, the Nephilim and the Elioud, through continual breeding with humans or their demonic possession of a human body (Recall they are angelic, thus having the power to make their dwelling place in such), gave way to psychopaths, sub-humans with no conscience whose only intent is to notarize themselves while shattering people's lives in the wakes of destruction they leave behind so they can be seen as God—again, like the anti-Christ.

Still question my rationale? Exactly who are the "tares among the wheat" to which Jesus referred in the parable in Matthew 13?

Allow both to grow together until the harvest; and in the time of the harvest I will say to the reapers, "First gather up the tares and bind them in bundles to burn them up; but gather the wheat into my barn." (Mathew 13:30, emphasis mine)

Are the tares merely the unsaved, or those who have no the ability to become saved, as they have no conscience? Who, or what, is the grain in this parable? Who is the wheat? And furthermore, in the verse depicted below, who is bound during the harvest to be burned? (*cf.* v. 30) Read the parable closely, respective of the material presented thus far.

> The kingdom of heaven may be compared to <u>a man who sowed good seed</u> in his field. But while men were sleeping, <u>his enemy came and sowed tares also among the wheat, and went away.</u> But <u>when the wheat sprang up and bore grain, then the tares became evident also.</u> The slaves of the landowner came and said to him, 'Sir, did you not sow good seed in your field? How then does it have tares?' And he said to them, '<u>An enemy has done this</u>!' The slaves said to him, 'Do you want us, then, to go and gather them up?' But he said, 'No; for while you are gathering up the tares, you may uproot the wheat with them. <u>Allow both to grow together until the harvest</u>; and <u>in the time of the harvest I will say to the reapers, "First gather up the tares and bind them in bundles to burn them up; but gather the wheat into my barn.</u>" (Matthew 13:24-30, emphasis mine)

Still skeptical? Then, where did mankind derive the images depicted in Greek mythology? Yes, in those paintings and writings depicting hybrids of angelic beings and human beings you learned of in high school or college literature classes; half angelic, half human, and fully demonic—*of Satan.*

This "species" of beings, the psychopath, roams the earth today without conscience, but they are destined for eternity in hell tomorrow. They will be bound in bundles and burned, forever. (*cf.* Matthew 13:30) But as of today, this is whom, or I should say, this is *what*, I have dealt for more than a decade.

May we never become fool-hearty in our efforts to understand God and his ways. God uses the ungodly and the Godly to accomplish his will, even Satan and his angels; sometimes, even your family and friends. But may your pit never involve a psychopath. He may stalk you, peak in your windows, or sit outside your home and watch you as he formulates his next move against you. He may pen his unfounded evil rants against you as components of his smear campaign, then send his lies to everyone who may listen; or seek to maliciously denigrate you in the face of your colleagues or clients, with evidence only substantiating the contrary. He may orchestrate situations, then play the victim. Again. Or, because he has no respect for humans, he may try to cut you with a knife, as he plays the role of victim, of course. Or have you put in jail under glaring falsehoods, lies, and corruption only the satanic can bring. He may orchestrate humanly foolish events, even when such events sometimes work against them, just to swing the pendulum of power back to himself, all so he and his can essentially be worshipped by those who know better, yet worship nonetheless.

Or, he may viciously ostracize your children from your family through his manipulative powers with others he controls, perhaps lock your children in their rooms day and night, with no relief except restroom breaks; even force them to eat alone in their rooms day and night with no human contact for weeks on end without your knowing. Or take them far away on vacation, only to lock one of them in the hotel room every day, all day, as a young child, for a week while everyone else is gone ten or twelve hours each day, literally, as he refuses to allow her to enjoy any activities that resembled a vacation. He may even physically beat up your children, literally, maybe even his own, then play the victim in front of the so-called authorities—again. Or he may strip your female children down naked as developed teenagers to view their physical "development," as if this is a role fathers should fulfill with teenage daughters.

He will accuse you of evils only he could envision, let alone do, a classic trait of a psychopath. He may completely disown his own, negating any resemblance to even secular parenthood while positioning himself as the picture of Godly fatherhood as he plays the role of victim over and over and over, especially anterior to those with the power to alter his dark courses of action.

He may. He will. And he did. But rest assured, friend, psychopaths spend eternity in hell with their own pit master, Lucifer himself, the keeper of darkness. How can they not? They have no conscience, *the very vehicle through which human beings distinguish right from wrong*. And, they know no right, and they know no wrong. They care nothing of social norms, let alone sin— God, or God's will; they are psychopaths. And when God comes for them, and he will, he will have no mercy on these serpents of darkness. The shaft will be separated from the wheat, bundled, and burned. Rest assured, "The wicked plots against the righteous, and gnashes at him with his teeth. The Lord laughs at him, for he sees his day coming." (Psalms 37:12-13)

Perhaps some wisdom from the world's two leading authorities on psychopathy can shed clinical insight into the darkness within this sub-human, the psychopathic being. Let us begin with Dr. Martha Stout, a former Harvard researcher and leading authority on psychopathy.

> Imagine, if you can, not having a conscience, none at all, no feelings of guilt or remorse no matter what you do, no limiting sense of concern of the well-being of strangers, friends, or even family members. Imagine no struggles with shame, not a single one in your whole life, no matter what kind of selfish, lazy, harmful, or immoral action you had taken. And pretend that the concept of responsibility is unknown to you, except as a burden others seem to accept without question, like gullible fools. Now add to this strange fantasy the ability to conceal from other people that your psychological makeup is radically different from theirs. Since everyone simply assumes that conscience is universal among human beings, hiding the fact that you are conscience-free is nearly effortless. You are not held back from any of your desires by guilt or shame, and you are never confronted by others for your cold-

bloodedness. The ice water in your veins is so bizarre, so completely outside of their personal experience that they seldom even guess at your condition. In other words, you are completely free of internal restraint, and your unhampered liberty to do just as you please, with no pangs of conscience, is conveniently invisible to the world. You can do anything at all.[43]

Dr. Robert Hare is an emeritus professor of psychology at the University of British Columbia, where he focused his research and other scholarly and clinical activities on psychopathy. He is, in fact, the developer of the single most definitively used instrument through which psychopaths are distinguished, the PCL-R. Concurrently, Dr. Hare also serves as the president of Darkstone Research Group, the world's most prominent authority on psychopathy, and an organization with a name that speaks to the wickedness associated with his investigations into the mind of Satan.

---

[43] Stout, M. (2005). The sociopath next door: The ruthless vs. the rest of us." Broadway Books, New York.

In Dr. Hare's own words,[44] "Jeffrey Dahmer. Ted Bundy. Hannibal Lecter. These are the psychopaths whose stunning lack of conscience we see in the movies and in tabloids. [They] haunt our everyday lives at work, at home, and in relationships..." But, as Dr. Stout, notes, most psychopaths are not the Dahmers, Bundys, or Lecters of the world. They operate behind masks shielding their evil, outside their victims and their families; the four percent of the world that are psychopaths, remain unknown. And while the world may refer to them by the softened, more politically correct name of sociopath, there is "no difference between a sociopath and psychopath." They are, in fact, "one in the same."[45]

Placing the evils associated with these beings in more definitive perspective, there are but two ways with which to deal with a psychopath, or at least as I have witnessed through my personal experiences, coupled with that of well over two hundred personal accounts I have studied. Run, and avoid every contact and every communication with a psychopath—*at all cost.* Or two, prepare for death, yours or his—and likely yours. He had just as

---

[44] Hare, R. (1994). This charming psychopath; how to spot predators before they attack. Psychology Today.

[45] Stout, M. (n.d.). Martha Stout interview. Living Heroes.

soon bludgeon you to death with a dull kitchen knife as he had look at you with his eyes of steel; and indeed, when given the choice, he will choose the former: he will bludgeon you to death. As such, you never, ever, befriend or attempt to help a psychopath, lest a darkness fall upon you in a way you can never imagine, let alone grasp. In the process, someone is likely to die.

As Dr. Hare continues, "All the reading in the world cannot immunize you from the devastating effects of psychopaths. Everyone, including the experts, can be taken in, conned, and left bewildered by them. A good psychopath can play a concerto on anyone's heart strings." Again, run; or prepare yourself for death, for as Dr. Hare describes such wickedness, "psychopaths are social predators, and like all predators, they are looking for feeding grounds." Or similarly, as God describes the psychopath's master, "...your adversary... prowls about you like a roaring lion, seeking someone to devour." (1 Peter 5:8)

And while you run, or prepare for death, "Be aware who the victim is [and who it is not]. Psychopaths often give the impression that it is they who are suffering and that the victims are to blame for their misery." It is part of their innate super-passive aggressive state of entitled mind. As the world's leading expert on psychopaths, Dr. Hare, sates, "Don't waste your sympathy on them." "The more you give in, the more you will be taken advantage of by the psychopath's insatiable appetite for power and control." They do not love you, nor will they love you. They can't; they are psychopaths. As Dr. Hare surmised, "A psychopath can use words like, 'I love you,' but it means nothing more than if he said, 'I'll have a cup of coffee.'"[46]

But as with most human beings, not to be confused with psychopaths who represent Satan in the flesh and who are not the least human, we long to help those we perceive in need, but again, woe to the fool who tries to help the psychopath, or tries to love a psychopath. Woe to the fool who gives these sub-humans the time of day, for even a second. Your pending destruction awaits.

"Here is the crux: Psychopaths don't feel they have psychological or emotional problems, and they see no reason to change their behavior to conform with societal standards they do not agree with." Moreover, as Dr. Hare continues, "Don't expect... changes. [The] personality of [a] psychopath is "carved in stone."

---

[46] Hare, R. (1994). This charming psychopath; how to spot predators before they attack. Psychology Today.

"There is nothing you can do [that] will produce fundamental, sustained changes in how they see themselves or others." Thus, as Dr. Hare states, "Cut your losses." Run, or prepare for death.

The psychopath, friend, will spend eternity in hell. Of this I am certain. They are not human. They give the appearance of such, but they are nothing but Lucifer in clothes.

After more than a decade of dealing with such darkness, a darkness with such grotesqueness, knowing their eventual place of eternal residence in the fiery pits of hell and damnation is the only solitude I have. He is from Satan, he is *of Satan*, and he answers to Satan. *And to Satan will he return.* He must. He has no conscience. Thus, he has not the ability to accept Christ, nor will he ever be desirous of such foolishness. To hell he will spend eternity. Amen, and Amen. Let Charles Spurgeon rest the real victim assured, "There is no injustice in the grace of God. God is as just when He forgives a believer as when He casts a sinner into hell." Besides, "if God did not spare angels when they sinned, but cast them into hell and committed them to pits of darkness, reserved for judgment," certainly he will cast into the pits of darkness one of Satan's own (*cf.* 2 Peter 4). So, to hell the psychopath will spend eternity—forever. Every psychopath.

Again, every psychopath. Man, woman, and child. And may their torture be merciless, especially the day they cry out to Jesus, *"You are the Son of God."* (*cf.* Mark 3:11) And let the saints rejoice!

To every reader of this text, may you never understand my inadvertent dealings into the dark world of psychopathy. I would go as far as to guess some of you skimmed the last few pages due to the grotesque description of these dark forces, or the fact that no matter how badly you wanted to believe these words in print, you just could not. Or, you may know full well what it is like to deal with evil of this magnitude—but likely, you do not, and moreover, hopefully, you never will. Never willingly offer any support or communication—of any kind—to the psychopath, no matter the relationship. Yes, you are kind-hearted; God made you that way. And perhaps you only want the best for them. God made you that way, as well. They may be a stranger, or family member, but woe to you, friend, for your blessings of yesterday will turn into your curses of today, and it will be far worse than the words herein allow me to describe. That, friend, I promise you.

Thus, may your ignorance on issues such as these remain just that, ignorance; as "psychopaths view any social exchange as a feeding opportunity, a test of wills in which, there can only be one winner. Their motives are to manipulate and take, ruthlessly and without remorse."[47] So may your ignorance reign high, friend, because, "...in much wisdom there is much grief, and increasing knowledge results in increasing pain." (Ecclesiastes 1:18)

The wake of destruction left by a psychopath is without equal. And it is forever, until God finally intervenes and sends him to his own place of torture. Crossing paths with a psychopath is liken to Satan's plot against Job. Callous. Constant. Raw. Relentless. Just evil. But for those few reading my words who have been in the crosshairs of a psychopath, take comfort only with God's word, for you comfort is not found elsewhere. "For the ruthless will come to an end, and the scorner will be finished. Indeed, all who are intent on doing evil will be cut off; who cause a person to be indicted by a word...and defraud the one in the right with meaningless arguments." (Isaiah 29:20-21) "Behold, the day of the Lord is coming, cruel, with fury and burning anger, to make the land a desolation; and *He will exterminate its sinners from it;*" (Isaiah 13:9) but as for today, this day, may your circumstances *never* dictate your theology, for that day, friend,

---

[47] Hare, R. (1993). Without conscience: The disturbing world of the psychopaths among us. Guilford Press. New York.

that day of extermination; it may delay, but it will never falter. Amen.

Obviously, enduring pits such as mine alters one's thinking, usually substantially. It did mine. It did my family's. And the change is permanent. Then again, as C. S. Lewis surmised, "We are not necessarily doubting that God will do the best for us; we are wondering how painful the best will turn out to be." As for me personally, my experiences in the pit have re-shaped me in ways that are not all positive. Overall, positive, maybe, but to say positive in even most ways would be a lie disguised as a stretch.

I accepted Christ as my personal savior 41 years ago and have served him faithfully, yet after involuntarily enduring the pit for more than a decade my questions regarding the ways of God now far outnumber my answers. As a somewhat weak secular comparison, the more I learned through my doctoral education, in both programs, the more I discovered that I did not know. And while the things I know regarding engineering, economic systems, statistics, and decision science are quite extensive, I have yet to scratch the surface in any one of these fields, let alone the surfaces at the intersections of those fields. Such is my spiritual life, especially following my worst days in the pit. The more I discovered of God, the less I believe I knew. Then again, this is a derivative of growth, spiritual, intellectual, or otherwise. But as for spiritual growth on this level, it comes at a supreme cost. In retrospect, perhaps I should have remained content on the sidelines.

Staying any biblical evidence to the contrary, the God I currently know is not the God I knew. In fact, he is far from it, and to be completely honest, I do not like everything I now know of God. But he is God, and I am not. My ways are not always his; hence, the pit. Thus, to be a seasoned Christian, to be one fairly well versed in his ways, often seems juxtaposed to my struggles of really knowing God.

Comparatively, it is similar to our handling of the relationship between Jesus and God in recent years. Statistically, that relationship is perfect, with a correlation coefficient of +1.0, if you will, but we treat that relationship as if it were -1.0, or inverse; at polar extremes, operating as opposing forces, with God on one end and Jesus on the other. For example, in decades past we heard from our pulpits less of Jesus and more of God; we heard more of God's damnation and less of Jesus' love. And we accepted Christ as our savior to spare ourselves from that damnation—or, what in reality is eternity in the pits of hell. Today, we most often hear only of Jesus' love, so subsequently we accept Christ for "what he can do for me." Of course, God's damnation and Jesus' love are one in the same, as what we see as God's destruction in our lives is actually his love for us. How could I love my children without disciplining them, guiding them, shaping them—and holding them? As John Wesley, the founder of Methodism, postulated, "What one generation tolerates, the next generation embraces." Friend, God doesn't tolerate, not for long.

Our problem today is that we want to be held, to be loved— *conditionally*, without stern discipline, definitive guidance, and continuous shaping. In reality, however, the God we want is not the God who is. He is in fact not the God we hear of on Sunday mornings, at least not only the Jesus we hear of on Sunday mornings. Oh, he is that, but he is so much more, and he is willing to completely destroy you for you to know him, and to know him, you must completely yield to him... "So that you will know that I am God." What an erroneous mess we have made in our attempt to shift this paradigm from the God who is to the God we want.

No, may my pit never be your pit.

As you enter your particular pit, that medium through which God will discipline you, guide you, and shape you, you may not realize that you have entered, as entrance into the pit is not always obvious. For some, the entrance may smell of sweetness, paved with fine silver, and be subtle. For others, the entrance may be abrupt, immediate, and without warning. In any regard, you may see your entrance as only temporary, something you can navigate with some effort. After all, by this point in your life you are a seasoned Christian who has weathered many, many storms, as only very seasoned Christians enter pits. The new Christian, weak Christian, or run of the mill Sunday go-to-meeting Christian could never weather the pit; thus, the reason God uses relatively cushy means of shaping them.[48] You, friend, have been chosen; you have been set aside. God has extended you an invitation to know him deeply, and knowing him at these depths only occurs through the pit. Hear me again. Knowing God at these depths only occurs through the pit. Nowhere else.

But woe to the undiscerning and discerning alike; this is not a passing storm. To know God at this depth is to be broken—

---

[48] Subsequently, they will never know God as you. Whether such is positive or negative, I suppose, is not only ambiguous, but debatable.

fractured, fragmented, and defeated. Completely. The pit is there to break you, to show you who you are relative to whose you are, to measure you against a rubric you never knew existed, among other reasons that will forever remain unknown to you. You, friend, are about to be defeated, over and over, something completely foreign to what you have known, and more eerily, what you have heard during your Sunday morning dose of feel-good. And make no mistake about it; God has no reservations in destroying one of his children if it accomplishes his ultimate objectives, even to the point of death. You will not weather this storm well. You will endure your pit alone, with little to no prior training or preparation relative to the challenges of your pit. In fact, given the simultaneous complexities associated with the pit, even the best operations researcher could not develop the most sophisticated algorithms through which to navigate. However, there are some general lessons that apply when in the pit, lessons you will learn to hold dearly as your stay in the pit is extended time and time again. In the interim, remember, there are no winners in the pit; only those who endure.

1. **The pit master controls the pit.** You do not control the pit; but neither does the pit control you, at least theoretically. However, you do not control your stay in

the pit, nor do you control the cost of staying in the pit. You remain captive of the pit to endure the ever-changing cost of staying in the pit until the pit master allows you to leave the pit. And the longer you struggle against the ways of the pit master, the longer you remain in the pit. As such, adapt to the ways of the pit master, for to resist the ways of the pit master is futile.

2. **The pit is not always deserved, but it is always intentional.** You may see nothing in your past that makes you a candidate for an extended stay in the pit, or maybe you do. Either way, buckle up, for your stay in the pit will be merciless. In fact, if your stay is not consistently merciless, you are not in the pit. However, be reminded that while your stay in the pit may not be deserved, the pit master placed you in the pit for reasons likely beyond your current comprehension such that the greater good of his will can be served, which should not necessarily to be likened as the greater good of your will.

3. **The pit is not a sustainer of life.** Subsequently, you must get out of the pit as quickly as possible, but recall, you do not control the pit, so you must yield to the ways of the pit imposed by the pit master if you hope to ever exit the pit.

4. **You are alone in the pit.** While you may have heard of people being in the pit, they have never been in your pit. This pit is yours; the pit master designed it especially for you because you are special, so do not expect people to understand your pit. They will not. Your suffrage will be in silence, and it will be alone. You will endure the pit with little help or counsel from even former or recovering pit dwellers. Most often, even God will leave you alone to wrestle in silence, but remember, the teacher is always quiet during the test. However, be mindful; the sooner you bend your knees in complete and final submission to ways of the pit master, the sooner you will leave the pit.

5. **The pit is not meant to be liked.** Conversely, the pit is meant to be endured. Further, understand that the pit is not about refining you as a precious stone. The pit is about beating you into submission to the ways of the pit master.

6. **Expect to appear as a fool to those who have never endure the pit.** Most people never endure the pit; even most Christians never endure the pit. Thus, during and after your stay in the pit, accept the fact that you appear as a fool to nearly all others, from your first day in the pit

forward. But time and time again, side with the pit master, though with him, life is egregious. Without him, there is no exit.

7. **Expect life in the pit to have many unforeseen turns.** With little help or counsel from former or recovering pit dwellers, you will regularly experience struggles you never knew existed, yet alone experienced. Worse, you will likely experience simultaneous struggles, as if being taunted by the pit master. And just when you find yourself moving closer to leaving the pit, another unexpected and likely undeserved trial will knock you lower in the pit than you knew existed. Thus, your struggles in the pit will worsen without warning, making the pit nearly unbearably deep and wide, perhaps so deep and wide that no man should have to endure.

8. **The pit master does not care who you were in your past life.** Any prior accomplishments, including any former storms you weathered, are of no value to the pit master while you are in the pit, unless of course he deems it appropriate to use any strengths acquired through past accomplishments against you; and he will. Expect any past accomplishments, especially any successfully

navigated trials, to serve merely as precursors to even greater trials.

9. **The fact that you successfully navigated the last trial orchestrated by the pit master is no guarantee you will successfully navigate the next trial.** Expect to fail over and over during your stay in the pit, but remember, failure to you is not necessarily seen as failure to the pit master. Most often, failure is exactly what the pit master ordained.

10. **You do not have to understand the ways of the pit master to obey the pit master.** Attempting to understand the ways of the pit master is futile; most efforts will be in vain and only serve to prolong your stay in the pit as you attempt to understand. Besides, if you understood the ways of the pit master, you would likely develop schemes to overcome his ways, altogether negating any growth associated with the pit. So while in the pit, obedience must always trump understanding. Understanding, if it comes, comes later.

11. **Do not expect to fully overcome the pit.** The pit master is smarter than that; the trials orchestrated by the pit master are meant to have a profound and permanent impact on your life. Thus, the pit will alter your future

forever. Who you are, what you desire, possibly everything about you. So, you can hate the pit, and sometimes hate the pit master, but yield to the ways of the pit master if you plan to ever exit the pit.

12. **When hurt, sadness, loneliness, anger, ambiguity, doubt, and strife overtake you in the pit, refer to item one above.**

The pit is a place few people enter and even fewer survive. The key to surviving the pit is not to win; it is to endure. There are no winners. You will lose nearly every battle. Winning is reserved for baseball games. Endurance will be the only winning you know. You will be beaten to a fine pulp, becoming a fragment of who you were in your previous life, barely recognizable, but you will have endured.

If you enter the pit, may you do so with trepidation.

Herbert M Barber, Jr, PhD, PhD

Search for Significance

He stands there alone, awaiting his suitor. Who will seek me, he says, for here am I. Yet so few will ever realize significance because so few seek to experience God for who he is. So for most, there will be no significance. We will leave this world as we came in—with nothing. Indeed, "The harvest is plentiful, but the workers are few." (Matthew 9:37)

Significance is not beyond the grasp of every man and woman; it stands ready to be grasped. Of these words, I am confident. But so few will leave this life with it. Oh, many will leave having earned significance in the world as we know it. Piles of toys with dust on them. But toys do not equate to significance, or crowns, in eternity. So maybe we should be so bold as to suggest that few will enter eternal life with God saying, "Well done good and faithful servant," (Matthew 25:23) because few of us will ever really seek him for who he is, for such mandates that we fully lay down our lives in complete submission to a god we have never touched, never heard, and never seen. Our submission only begins when all avenues have been exploited and failed, again; when there is no other alternative.

As we resist complete submission to God, however, it is as if we have buried our talents, gifts, experiences, and educations for that which we call, the material, the tangible, that which we can see—and perhaps more importantly, that which others can see. The perishable. The dust. But in our quest to attain something of which we approve, or others approve, we sacrifice what could have been—and what will be in eternity. We cash in significance with God for what has become our god. We throw it all away, and the "could have beens" are never realized.

For it is just like a man about to go on a journey, who called his own slaves and entrusted his possessions to them. To one he gave five talents, to another, two, and to another, one, each according to his own ability; and he went on his journey. Immediately the one who had received the five talents went and traded with them, and gained five more talents. In the same manner the one who had received the two talents gained two more.

But he who received the one talent went away, and dug a hole in the ground and hid his master's money.

Now after a long time the master of those slaves came and settled accounts with them. The one who had received the five talents came up and brought five more talents, saying, "Master, you entrusted five talents to me. See, I have gained five more talents." His master said to him, "Well done, good and faithful slave. You were faithful with a few things; I will put you in charge of many things; enter into the joy of your master."

Also the one who had received the two talents came up and said, "Master, you entrusted two talents to me. See, I have gained two more talents." His master said to him, "Well done, good and faithful slave. You were faithful with a few things; I will put you in charge of many things; <u>enter into the joy of your master</u>."

And the one also who had received the one talent came up and said, "Master, I knew you to be a hard man, reaping where you did not sow and gathering where you scattered no seed. And I was afraid, and went away and hid your talent in the ground. See, you have what is yours."

But his master answered and said to him, "You wicked, lazy slave, you knew that I reap where I did not sow and gather where I scattered no seed. Then you ought to have put my money in the bank, and on my arrival I would have received my money back with interest. Therefore, take away the talent from him, and give it to the one who has the ten talents."

For to everyone who has, more shall be given, and he will have an abundance; but from the one who does not have, even what he does have shall be taken away. <u>Throw out the worthless slave into the outer darkness; in that place there will be weeping and gnashing of teeth</u>. (Matthew 25:14-30; emphasis mine)

Do you think God was serious about Christians using their God-given gifts and talents in a manner he deems appropriate? I think it is safe to assume that answer is a resounding yes. Nonetheless, we go about our days on earth leveraging our gifts and talents for our personal benefit with little realistic consideration to his will. In so doing, unfortunately, for most believers, worldly accomplishments will result in the sum total of all significance captured.

In statistics and econometrics, we go to elaborate lengths to probabilistically determine whether a phenomenon or relationship is significant, and it is a subject of importance to us. If a phenomenon, relationship, or the like is considered statistically significant, we have determined through some rubric, be it alpha levels, effect sizes, F-tests, chi-squared, or more advanced statistic, the degree to which the phenomenon or relationship is likely due to chance.[49] In our personal lives, however, our significance on earth can be expressed as a measure of the relationship we have with God, and our relationship with God often can be expressed as the relationship between our dependency on God and our material success in life. Certainly, this relationship does not always hold true, but often it does. Regardless as to how we define success, the more successful we become through our own means and schemes, the less likely we are to become dependent on God, and thus, the weaker our

---

[49] In our personal lives, there is no such variable as chance, not if God is the sovereign, omnipresent person he claims.

relationship with God. And often, the less success we generate through our own talents, gifts, experiences, and educations, the greater our dependency on God. The relationship is inverse.[50] In lay terms, these variables often act in contrast with one another, and while this relationship certainly does not always hold true, it is worth consideration.

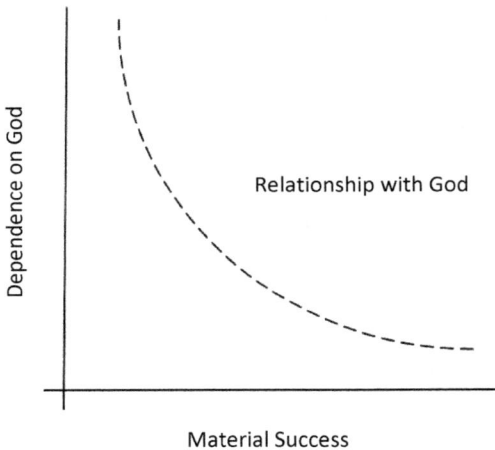

This overly simple relationship helps explain why we often see those who have acquired much in life struggle with their relationship with Christ, and more specifically, to completely yield

---

[50] More specifically, the relationship, at least as depicted here, is inverse with some measure of curvilinearity.

to his will. In my experience, this seems to hold particularly true with persons of very high intelligence. For example, many persons with earned doctorates have difficulty accepting Christ as their personal savior if such yielding did not occur prior to them earning their PhD. Like any doctor worth his salt, he has the intellectual ability to reason away his need to serve an unseen god—or a god of which he questions his very existence. Usually, accepting God exists on faith alone is simply not an idea a learned doctor will readily accept on faith alone, especially one educated in the mathematical sciences where theories must be proven quantitatively to offer any evidence of validity. Similar concepts apply to wealth, income, fame, and other variables we use to define success. Where there is no acknowledged need, there is no desire.

Regardless how one defines success, the same principal likely holds true. Jesus said so himself in Matthew 19:24.[51] "It is easier for a camel to go through the eye of a needle, than for a rich man to enter the kingdom of God." Conversely it explains why Mrs. Murphy, my childhood babysitter, had such a strong relationship

---

[51] There exist various opinions among scholars regarding the exact meaning of Matthew 19:24. However, the overall point Jesus was making appears to hold true in most opinions.

with Christ. She had so little, yet she attained great significance. Likewise, it explains why my father has attained great significance; because he never attempted to trump God's desires for his life with his desires for his life. Knowing that man cannot serve man and God, he chose the latter. (*cf.* Matthew 6:24) Of course, the funny thing about life is, young people are ready to set the world on fire, middle-aged people wonder if they ever will, and older people know that setting the world on fire is overrated, anyway. Significance is only realized through *Him*.

Subsequently, never before have I been so certain of Mathew 19:30. "...many who are first will be last; and the last, first." And for Daddy and people like him, what a day of celebration that will be! "Well done my good, faithful servant!" (Matthew 25:21) "Enter his gates with thanksgiving; and his courts with praise." (Psalms 100:4)

Who am I

To my children, Brandon and Natalie, who am I? Through the many difficult trials that have come my way, that single question I ponder. Who am I? The question gives rise to deep philosophical thought, prayer, reflection, and more prayer, with the question only being answered in trial?

When I was earning my first doctorate, my son Brandon, some four years old at the time, posed a deafening question to me as I tucked him into bed one night, something he and I relished as I was rarely home, always either at work or in school. All these years later, his question continues to silence me. "Daddy, when you finish being a doctor, will you be a daddy?" Only through the eyes of a child, as they say. And to this end, I ponder, who am I.

In the strangest of twists that are witnessed only by the fewest of Christians, Job fought to withstand the worst storm God had ever thrown against man, arguably, outside of killing him outright, and somehow survived. I too have battled storms, even the pit. Perhaps so have you.

It wasn't pretty for Job; neither was it pretty for me. Physically, psychologically, and emotionally, Job was ruined. But spiritually; Job was still there, as am I. Hanging on by a single thread, but somehow... there, nonetheless. And as with Job, through some never before experienced depth of my soul, I clamber on my knees to my destroyer, humbly and meekly, spent.

Who am I, that the Lord of all the earth would care to know my name, would care to feel my hurt?

Who am I, that the bright and morning star would choose to light the way for my ever-wandering heart?

Who am I, that the eyes that see my sin would look on me with love?

Who am I, that the voice that calmed the sea, would call out through the rain, and calm the storm in me?[52]

Who am I? *"I am Yours."* And I am insignificant.

---

[52] Casting Crowns. (2004). Who am I. Beach Street/Reunion/PLG

The man with a cross no longer controls his destiny.
He lost control when he picked up his cross. [Now], there is but
one thing he can do; move forward toward
his place of crucifixion.

A.W. Tozer

Herbert M Barber, Jr, PhD, PhD

.

Herbert M Barber, Jr, PhD, PhD is one of ten leading authorities in the world today who specializes in the measurement, analyses, modelling, and forecasting of econometric effect and causality large endeavors in industry and infrastructure have on financial and economic output, such as revenue, profit, GDP, personal income, job growth, and tax generation. He has conducted over 250 scientific and technological investigations involving the greater infrastructure-economics nexus. Additionally, he is well published in the scientific literature.

Dr. Barber is an avid speaker and writer regarding spiritual disobedience in America as it relates to the rise of decay within economic, political, and social constructs. Subsequently, he is an outspoken critic against the oppressive tyranny that has become increasingly prevalent in the United States, and has no problem substantiating his claims with rigorous quantitative analyses.

Complementing his experience, Dr. Barber holds five earned academic degrees, including a bachelor's degree, two master's degrees, and two doctorates, from Georgia Southern University, Florida State University, and Mississippi State University. Above all else, he is a child of God.